BIBLE TIME

with Kids

400+
Bible-based Activities to Use with Children

CINDY DINGWALL

Abingdon Press
Nashville

Bible Time with Kids

400+ Bible-based Activities to Use with Children

Copyright © 1997 by Cindy Dingwall

All rights reserved.
No part of this work, EXCEPT PUZZLES, PATTERNS, AND PAGES COVERED BY THE FOLLOWING NOTICE, may be reproduced or transmitted in any form or by any means, electronic or mechanical, including photocopying and recording, or by any information storage or retrieval system, except as may be expressly permitted by the 1976 Copyright Act or in writing from the publisher. Requests for permission should be addressed in writing to Abingdon Press, 201 Eighth Avenue South, Nashville, TN 37203.
This book is printed on recycled, acid-free paper.
ISBN 0-687-01043-8

Unless otherwise noted, Scripture quotations are from the New Revised Standard Version Bible. Copyright © 1989 by the Division of Christian Education of the National Council of the Churches of Christ in the USA. Used by permission.

ANY PUZZLE OR PATTERN may be reproduced for use in the local church or church school provided the following copyright notice is included:
From *Bible Time with Kids: 400+ Bible-based Activities to Use with Children*. © 1997 by Cindy Dingwall. Reprinted by permission.

98 99 00 01 02 03 04 05—10 9 8 7 6 5 4 3 2

MANUFACTURED IN THE UNITED STATES OF AMERICA

To the members of Church of the Incarnation. Their love and support continues to be an inspiration and source of strength to me.

CONTENTS

ACKNOWLEDGMENTS

Many thanks to:

The pastors of Church of the Incarnation:

Larry Hilkemann for encouraging me to assume leadership responsibilities within our church.

The late Jim Reid for appointing me as a Shepherd.

Louise Mahan for encouraging me to "find a solid place to stand, trust in God to prepare something new for me," and then challenging me to fly.

Tom Ostrander for his prayers and support during a time of transition in my life, for answering my myriad of questions, for providing explanations of theology, and for letting me use the computer concordance.

To the Sunday school staff for inviting me to present "special programs" for our children during their Sunday school time and for allowing me to teach during the summer months rather than the regular school year, so that I could enjoy being a member of the Incarnation Choir and sing during worship services.

To the members of my church Shepherd Group who endured many of these activities, so that I could find out if they worked. They are: Bill and Diane Blizek, Max and Eloise Brittain, Clint and Marge Cederlund, Audrey Cline, Dave and Cathy Coughlin, Art and Marian Gardiner, Margaret Gramley, Kevin and Laurie Hurtubise, Mike and Lesley Hurtubise, Frank and Connie Lee, Bill and Pat Mayhew, Lynn Schreiner, and Ethel Smith.

To the Youth Services Department of the Arlington Heights Memorial Library for help in more ways than I could ever imagine. They include: Jeanne Achenbach, Marsha Balster, Pat Craig, Barbara d'Ambrosio, Maureen Dudle, Mary Ferrini, Ruth Griffith, Fred Gross, Margaret Kennedy, Gloria Kries, Betty Lockwood, Mary Lucas, Judy Moskal, Erika Scherpf and Sara Zimmerman.

To the Palatine Public Library for providing a beautiful and peaceful setting in which to research and work.

To Bill Miller, my senior-year English teacher at Cary-Grove High School for recognizing my writing talent, teaching me to write properly, and, most of all, inspiring me to write.

To all my friends who kept telling me I could really do this.

To Abingdon Press who encouraged me in my first time endeavor of writing a book.

But most of all to God . . . who keeps taking my life into new, sometimes scary, yet fascinating directions—and always stays right beside me wherever we go.

INTRODUCTION

Bible Time with Kids is about children and adults sharing church activities, projects, and special events together.

Children and adults can glean many insights as we come together to share in the joy of God's love for us. Together we can grow in our Christian faith as we learn about God's love for us. We can delight in sharing activities together.

Everytime I come away from working with a group of children, I marvel at what I learn from them. Sharing activities with children helps us keep a fresh outlook on life. It keeps us young at heart. As we share our lessons of faith with children, we too grow and develop a deeper understanding of God.

My original intent upon joining my church was not to become involved with the children's programming. Since I was working professionally as a children's librarian, I felt the need to explore other opportunities for Christian service. At the time, I was very much involved in working with adults, which I found gratifying and rewarding. However, God had other plans for me. It took the encouragement of our pastor and the proddings of my friends to convince me that God wanted me involved in children's ministry. The comment that finally convinced me was made by a friend who said, "God has given you these gifts and talents for working with children. When God blesses us with such gifts, God expects us to glorify him by using them to the best of our ability."

And so it began—and it continues.

BIBLE PUZZLES

Children enjoy the challenge of completing puzzles. Included here are a variety of puzzles that highlight Bible stories, characters, and principles. They are designed to enhance the Bible stories included in this book.

Age suggestions are provided for each puzzle, however feel free to be flexible in using various puzzles with different age groups depending on the individual abilities of the children. Age groupings are: ages 3-6 (preschool, kindergarten); ages 6-8 (grades 1-2); ages 8-12 (grades 3-6).

Puzzles can be used in children's worship bulletins, children's church, Sunday school, Christian day care and school, and after-school programs. They can also be included on a special children's page in the church newsletter. Solutions are in the Appendix on pages 164-65.

HINTS

1. When working with children with different abilities, be prepared to offer assistance as needed. (Have children work in pairs, matching a more advanced child with one who has difficulty; work with the child[ren] yourself; or have a class aid.)

2. Have each child work on a segment of a puzzle, thus making it a class project; or work as a group on a puzzle.

3. For children who dislike doing puzzles, offer an alternative activity. (Draw a picture of your favorite character in the story; draw a picture of your favorite part of the story.)

4. Adapt puzzles to fit the needs and abilities of children in your class. (Fill in parts of the dot-to-dot activities for young children; fill in some of the coloring portions of coloring puzzles.)

5. If older children would prefer a simpler puzzle, let them try one of the puzzles for younger children. Young children who are ready may be given more challenging puzzles.

6. Use a copier to enlarge puzzles for children who have visual difficulties.

WHAT DID GOD CREATE?

Scripture: Genesis 1–2:3

Dot-to-Dot (Ages 3-6)

Connect the dots to discover something important that God created. Color it yellow. What is it? Why is it important?

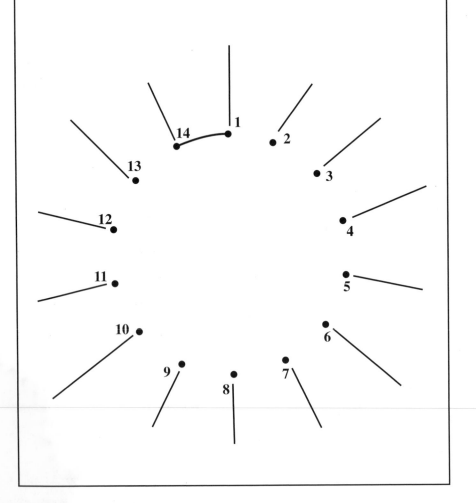

GOD'S CREATION

Scripture: Genesis 1–2:3, adapted

Hidden Pictures (Ages 6-8)

Can you find and color pictures of the things God created?

GOD CREATED

Scripture: Genesis 1–2:3

Crossword Puzzle (Ages 8-12)

Across
1. On the first day God created day and _____.
2. On the seventh day God _____.
3. God created fish and _____ on the fifth day.
4. On the _____ day, God created sun, moon, and stars.

Down
1. On the sixth day, God created _____ and people.
2. On the second day, God created sky and _____.
3. God created _____ on the third day.
4. _____ created the world.

Decorate your paper with pictures of things God created.

Write down the letters that are circled. Unscramble them to discover the message.

God said, "__ __ __ __ __ __ __."

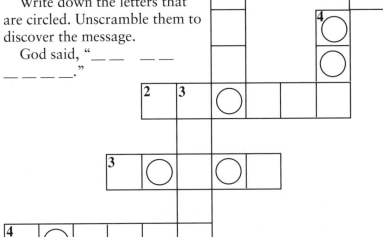

WHAT APPEARED IN THE SKY?

Scripture: Genesis 6–9

Dot-to-Dot (Ages 3-6)

Can you follow the numbers that connect the dots to make a picture of something in the Bible? Color your picture.

Things to talk about:
What is this a picture of?
Why is it special?

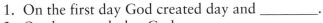

WHERE'S NOAH?

Scripture: **Genesis 6–9**

Hidden Picture (Ages 6-8)

Oh no! There are so many animals on the ark that Noah is lost. Can you locate him?

WHAT APPEARED?

Scripture: **Genesis 6–9**

Crossword Puzzle (Ages 8-12)

Use your Bible to find the answers to this puzzle.

Across
1. God told _____ to build an ark.
2. Noah filled the ark with _____.
3. Noah worked hard to _____ the ark.
4. When the _____ returned, she brought back an olive branch.
5. The ark floated on the _____ during the storm.

Down
1. It _____ for forty days.
2. The rain caused a big _____ that covered the entire earth.
3. Noah was six _____ years old when the flood occurred.

Illustrate your paper with pictures of animals from "Noah's Ark." Write the letters that are circled.

Unscramble them to answer this question: What appeared at the end of this story?

_____

What does it remind us of?

_____

HOW MANY ANGELS CAN YOU FIND?

Scripture: Genesis 28:10-22

Hidden Picture (Ages 3-5)

Color each angel you find in the clouds. How many are there?

I PROMISE

Scripture: Genesis 28:10-22

Shape Puzzle (Ages 6-8)

Color

Circles—Yellow	Squares—Orange
Rectangles—Green	Ovals—Pink

Unscramble the letters in each shape to see what words appear from the story. Use them to tell the story in your own words.

Circles: _____ Rectangles: _____

Squares: _____ Ovals: _____

Who promised to stay with Jacob wherever he went? _____
(Look for the shapes with stars to find the answer.)

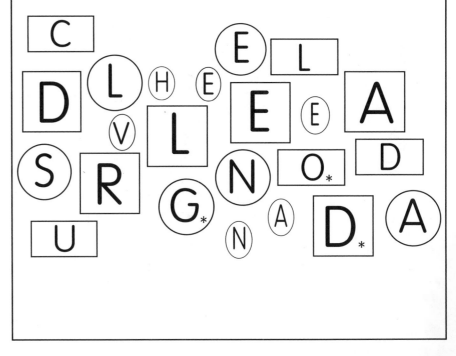

WHAT DID GOD PROMISE?

Scripture: Genesis 28:10-22

Hidden Message (Ages 8-12)

Circle every fourth letter to find the promise God made to Jacob.

What was the promise? __ ___ _____ ___ __

___ ____ _____ ____

___ _____ ___ __

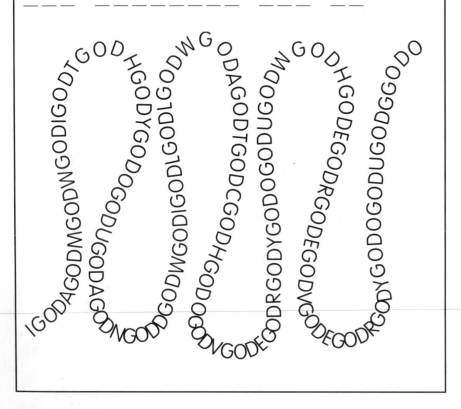

WHAT DID JOSEPH WEAR?

Scripture: Genesis 37:3

Dot-to-Dot (Ages 3-6)

Connect the dots to make a special picture. Then use many different colors to color your picture. What did you make?

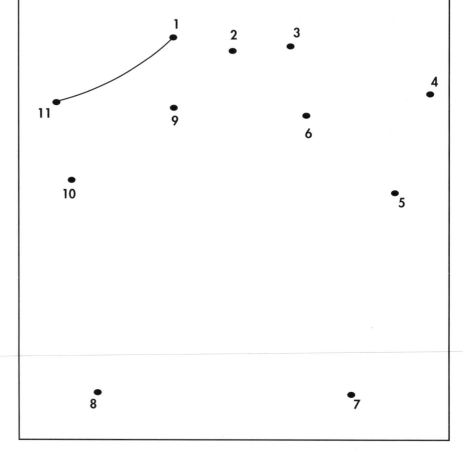

JOSEPH'S COAT

Scripture: Genesis 37:3

Coloring Puzzle (Ages 6-8)

Color:

B blue   Y yellow   R red

G green   O orange   P purple

What did you make? _____

WHO ARE WE?

Scripture: Genesis 35:23-26

Scrambled Words Puzzle (Ages 8-12)

Unscramble the letters to spell the names of important people in this story.

NEBUER __ __ __ Ⓞ __ __ __

MENSOI __ __ __ Ⓞ __ __

VEIL __ __ __ __

HUDAJ __ __ __ __ __

CHARAISA __ __ __ __ Ⓞ __ __ __

ULZEBUN __ __ __ __ __ __ __

EAIJBNNM __ __ __ Ⓞ __ __ __ __

NAD __ __ __

PHANTLAI __ __ __ __ __ __ __ __

ADG __ __ __

RESHA Ⓞ __ __ __ __ __

Who are these people? _____

Write down the circled letters. _____

What do they spell? _____

Who is this person? _____

WHERE DID THIS HAPPEN?

Scripture: **Exodus 20:1-17**

Dot-to-Dot (Ages 3-6)

Connect the dots to find out where Moses was when God gave him the Ten Commandments.

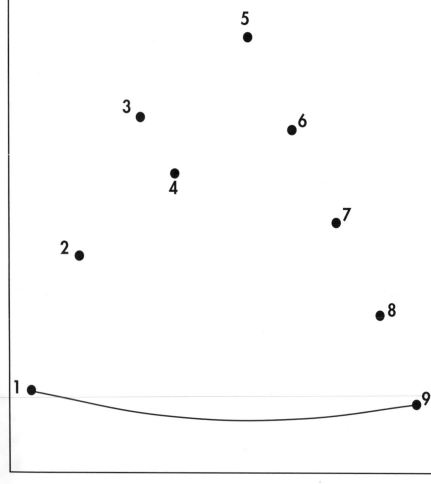

WHO DID GOD TELL?

Scripture: **Exodus 20:1-17**

Hidden Word Puzzle (Ages 6-8)

God gave this man important rules to share with us. They were called The Ten Commandments. Who did God share this important message with? Follow the path connecting the letters to find his name. _____

WHAT'S THE MESSAGE?

Scripture: Exodus 20:1-17, adapted

Scrambled Words and Sentences (Ages 8-12)

Can you unscramble these words and sentences?

LOUSJEA   DO   TON   EB

_____

SUE   ONT   DAB   DORWS   DO

_____

LIKL   TON   OD

_____

YLNO   DOG   WHIPSOR

_____

TON   OD   LSEAT

_____

RENTPAS   RONOH   RUOY

_____

OD   ONT   IEL

_____

NHORO   RRIAMGEA

_____

HURCCH   NO   OG   DAYSUN   TO

_____

GNITHS   WHOSRIP   TON   DO

_____

Now that you have unscrambled the words and sentences, see if you can put the sentences in the correct order to make

_____

WHAT ATE JONAH?

Scripture: Book of Jonah

Dot-to-Dot (Ages 3-6)

Connect the dots to make a picture. What is it? Color your picture.

WHAT ATE JONAH?

Scripture: Book of Jonah

Coloring Puzzle (Ages 6-8)

Color the spaces using the color key:

1—GRAY   3—PURPLE   5—BLUE   7—WHITE

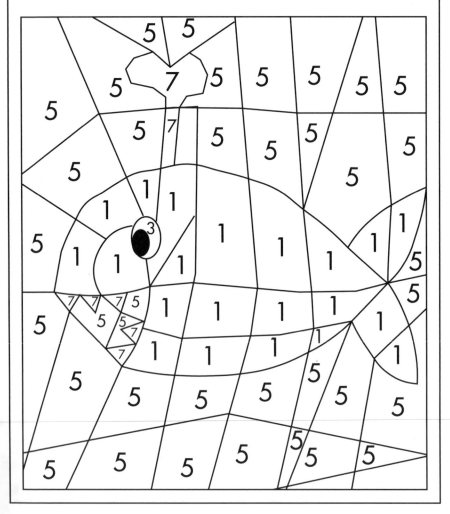

WHAT DOES GOD DO?

Scripture: Book of Jonah

Word Puzzle (Ages 8-12)

Use the words to fill in the missing letters to find an important message about God. Then look in the box to discover what that message is.

Nineveh	Storm	Love	Spit Out	Fear
Anger	Jonah	Three Days	Trouble	Sea
Whale	God	Prayed		

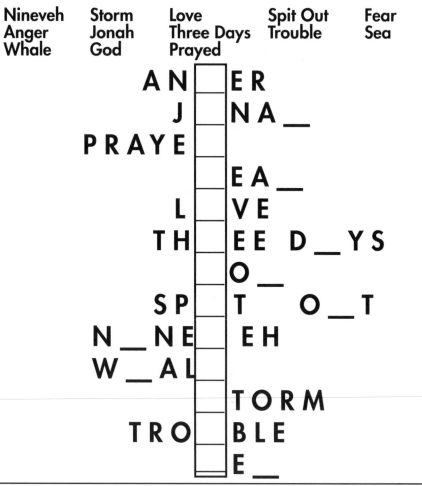

WHERE'S THE STAR?

Scripture: Luke 2:1-20

Hidden Picture (Ages 3-6)

Look at all of the stars in the sky. Can you find the star of Bethlehem that reminds us of when Jesus was born? Color it bright yellow.

THE ROAD TO BETHLEHEM

Scripture: Matthew 1:18-25 and Luke 2:1-20

Maze (Ages 6-8)

See if you can help Joseph and Mary get from Nazareth to Bethlehem. Why did they have to go to Bethlehem? What happened while they were there?

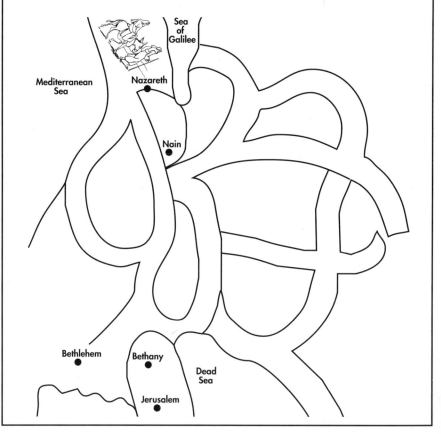

CHRISTMAS EVE

Scripture: **Matthew 1:18–2:12 and Luke 2:1-20**

Word Search (Ages 8-12)

Find the words from the WORD LIST in the puzzle. Draw a line through each word as you find it. Words go across or down. When you have located all of the words, there will be letters left over that spell a word from the Christmas story. Circle those letters to see what they spell.

```
J O S E P H L O V E
D G H J K O O A A B
O I E O I P R L W J
N F P U N E D L E E
K T H R G M A R Y S
E S E N B A B Y E U
Y T R E A N G E L S
H L D Y E G Y O U T
W I S E M E N H E A
M M E C H R I S T R
```

WORD LIST

Love	Joseph	Hope	Shepherds
Gifts	Wise Men	King	Manger
Awe	Baby	Lord	Mary
All	Angels	Me	Star
You	Journey	Jesus	Christ
Donkey			

Word: _____

Why is this word special?_____

_____

THE SERMON ON THE MOUNT

Scripture: **Matthew 5:3-12, adapted**

Fill It In (Ages 8-12)

Complete the puzzle. The circled letters spell a special Bible verse that is included in The Beatitudes. Use your Bible to help you. Look in Matthew 5:1-12.

1. Blessed are the __ __ __ Ⓞ in spirit.
2. For theirs is the kingdom of __ __ __ __ Ⓞ __ __
3. Ⓞ __ __ __ __ __ __ __ are they who mourn.
4. For they shall be __ Ⓞ __ __ __ __ __ __ __.
5. Blessed are the __ __ __ __ __
6. For they shall inherit the Ⓞ __ __ __ __.
7. Blessed are they who __ __ __ Ⓞ __ __ and thirst for righteousness,
8. For they shall be __ Ⓞ __ __ __ __ __.
9. Blessed are the __ __ __ Ⓞ __ __ __ __
10. For they shall have __ Ⓞ __ __ __.
11. Blessed are the pure in __ __ __ Ⓞ __ __,
12. For they shall see __ __ Ⓞ.
13. Blessed are the __ __ __ __ __ __ __ __ __
14. For they shall be called the __ __ __ Ⓞ __ __ __ Ⓞ of God.
15. Blessed are they who are persecuted for

    __ __ __ __ __ __ __ __ __ __ __ __ __ sake.
16. For theirs is the __ __ __ __ Ⓞ __ __ of __ __ Ⓞ __ __.
17. Blessed are __ __ __ when others shall hate you and persecute you and say bad things about you when you talk about __ __.

    Fill in the circled letters. Unscramble the special message.

    __ __ J __ __ __ __ __   __ __ __   __ __   __ __ __ __!

WHAT'S THE MESSAGE?

Scripture: Matthew 7:12, adapted

Shape Puzzle (Ages 8-12)

Use the color code to color the shapes. Each color spells a word. Together the words will make a special message. Color lightly, so the letters can be seen. Color them in the order listed below. As you finish coloring each word, unscramble it and write it in spaces below.

Triangle—yellow   Diamond—light blue   Heart—pink
Half Circle—blue   Crescent—orange   Square—red
Circle—green   Oval—gray   Blob—blue-green
Rectangle—lavender   Star—purple

___ ___ ___ ___ ___ ___ ___ ___ ___ ___

___ ___ ___ ___ ___ ___ ___ ___ ___ ___ ___ ___

___ ___ ___ ___ ___ ___ ___ .

WHAT DID JESUS SAY?

Scripture: Matthew 6:9-13, adapted

Scrambled Sentences Puzzle (Ages 8-12)

Can you unscramble these sentences and put them in the correct order?

For thine is the kingdom, and the power, and the glory forever.

On earth as it is in heaven.

And lead us not into temptation

Hallowed would be thy name.

Amen.

Give us this day our daily bread.

Thy will be done.

Our Father, who art in heaven.

And forgive us our sins, as we forgive other sinners.

But deliver us from evil.

Thy kingdom come.

This is known as _____.

WHAT DID THEY EAT?

Scripture: Matthew 14:15-21; Mark 6:35-44; Luke 9:12-17; John 6:5-14

Dot-to-Dot (Ages 3-6)

Connect the dots to see what the 5,000 people ate.

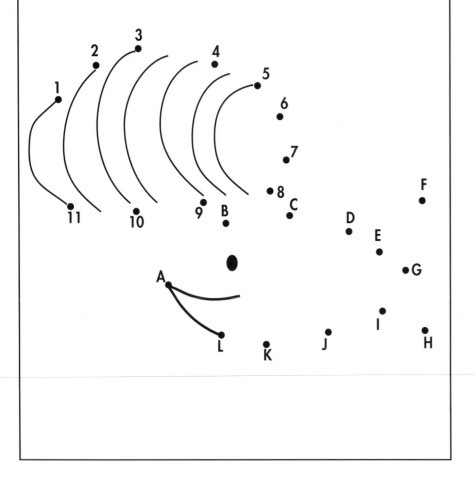

WHERE ARE THEY?

Scripture: Matthew 14:15-21; Mark 6:35-44; Luke 9:12-17; John 6:5-14

Hidden Pictures (Ages 6-8)

The fishes and loaves are lost! Can you find them? Circle them. How many fish did you find? _____
How many loaves of bread did you find? _____

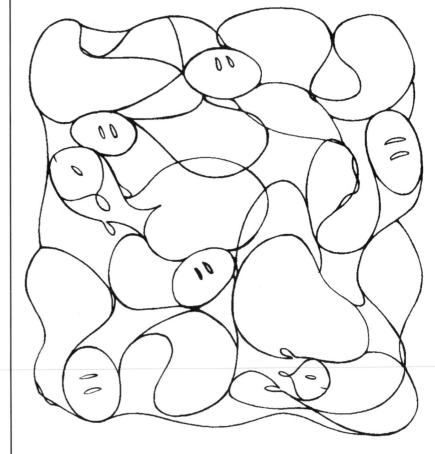

WHAT HAPPENED?

Scripture: **Matthew 14:15-21; Mark 6:35-44; Luke 9:12-17; John 6:5-14**

Word Puzzle (Ages 8-12)

Fill in the missing letters to spell important words from this story. When all of the letters are used, look in the box to discover the message.

Here are the words you will use.

**Disciples
Blessed
Shared
Hungry
Crowd
Five
Sea
Everyone
Enough
Prayed
Bread
Feeds
Fish
Fed
Followed
Heaven
Loaves
Jesus
Grass
Ate
Up
Us**

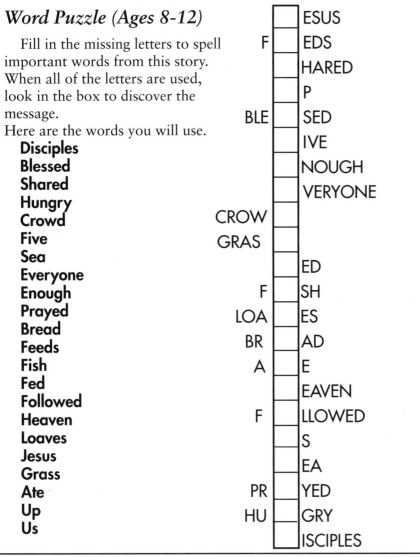

	ESUS
F	EDS
	HARED
	P
BLE	SED
	IVE
	NOUGH
	VERYONE
CROW	
GRAS	
	ED
F	SH
LOA	ES
BR	AD
A	E
	EAVEN
F	LLOWED
	S
	EA
PR	YED
HU	GRY
	ISCIPLES

JESUS HEALED MANY PEOPLE

Scripture: **Matthew 8:1-4, 14-17, 9:1-8, 18-22, 27-34 and others**

Dot-to-Dot (Ages 3-6)

Connect the dots to find out what Jesus used to heal people. Jesus often placed his _____ upon people when he healed them.

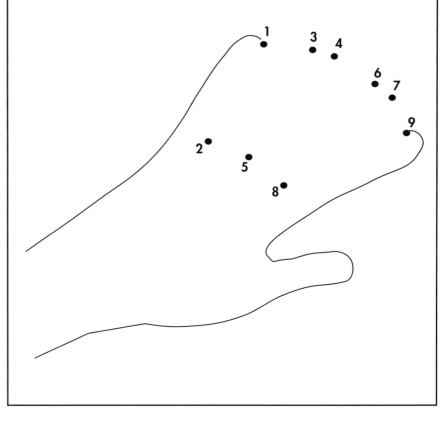

WHO DID JESUS HEAL?

Scripture: Matthew 8:1-4, 14-17, 9:1-8, 18-22, 27-34 and others

Crossword Puzzle (Ages 8-12)

Use a Bible to find the missing words

ACROSS
1. Jesus healed a man with _____. (Matthew 8:1-4)
2. Jesus healed a man who was _____ and lying on a mat unable to move.
(Matthew 9:1-8)
3. As he was healing the man with leprosy, Jesus said, "Be made _____!"
   (Matthew 8:3)
4. Jesus healed two men who were possessed by _____. (Matthew
8:28-34)

DOWN
1. Jesus healed Peter's mother-in-law who had a _____. (Matthew 8:14-15)
2. Jesus healed a man who was _____. (Matthew 20:29-34)
3. Jesus healed _____ daughter who had been close to death.
   (Mark 5:21-24)
4. A woman who had been _____ _____ for eighteen years
was healed by Jesus. (Luke 13:10-13)

Draw pictures that show what Jesus did.
Write the letters that are circled. _____
These healings are some of the _____ Jesus performed.
(Unscramble the letters to find the missing word.)

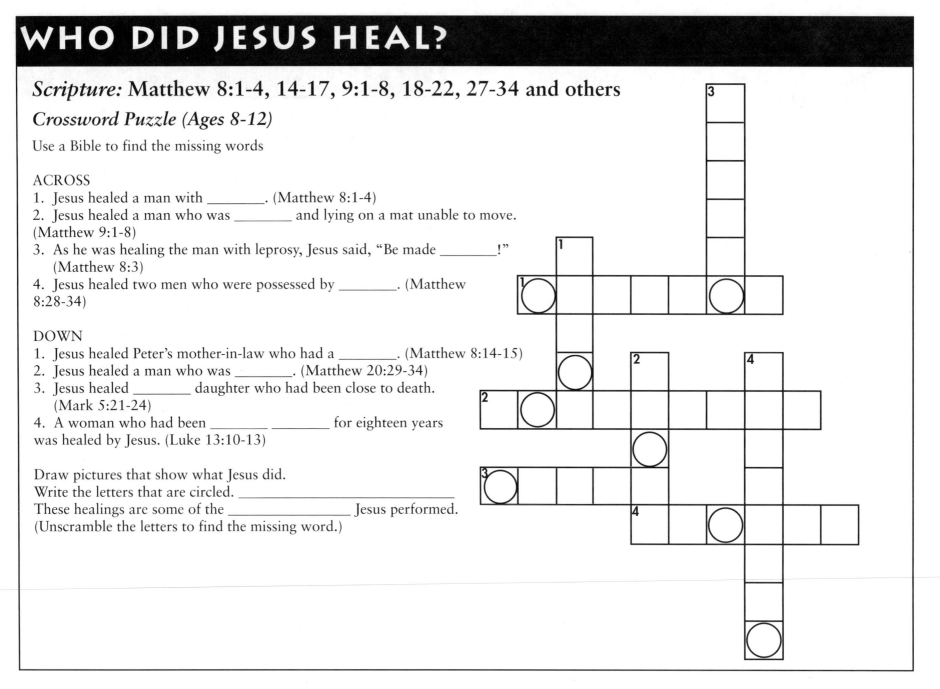

WHAT DID JESUS DO?

Scripture: **Matthew 8:1-4, 14-17, 9:1-8, 18-22, 27-34, and others**

Shape Puzzle (Ages 6-8)

Color the shapes in the order listed below. As you finish coloring each shape, write the words in the spaces below to spell a special message.

Circles—Red	Squares—Orange
Ovals—Green	Rectangles—Blue

_ _ _ _ _   _ _ _ _ _   _ _ _ _ _ .

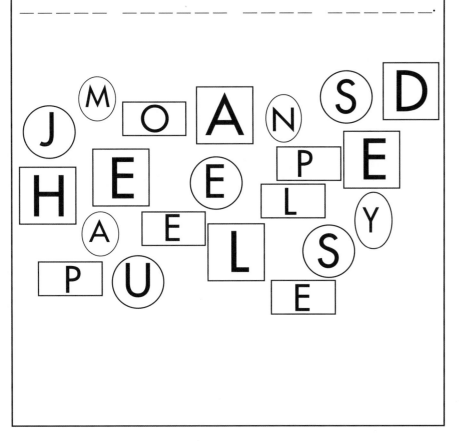

CAN YOU FIND THE DISCIPLES IN THE BOAT?

Scripture: **Matthew 14:22-36**

Hidden Picture (Ages 3-6)

Use the color code to color the squares and find the disciples.
Color:

G—Gray	O—Brown	B—Blue

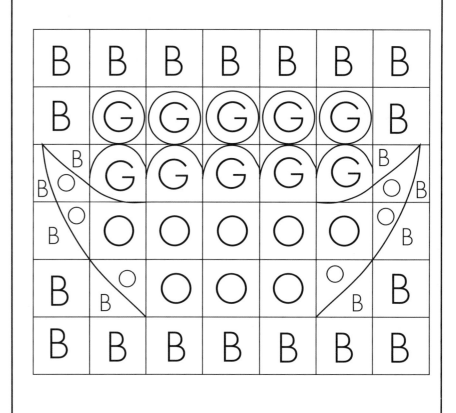

LOOK AT PETER!

Scripture: Matthew 14:22-36

Maze (Ages 6-8)

Can you help Peter walk across the water to Jesus? Draw a line through the open waves that lead Peter to Jesus. Why did Jesus ask Peter to walk on the water with him?

LOOK WHAT JESUS DID!

Scripture: Matthew 14:22-36

Word Puzzle (Ages 8-12)

Fill in the missing letters from the words listed below. When you are finished, you will discover another one of Jesus' miracles in the box.

Here are the words you will use.

Faith
Us
Me
Boat
Afraid
God
Sink
Disciples
Lord
Jesus
Water
Waves
Come
Sea
Peter
Walking
Wind

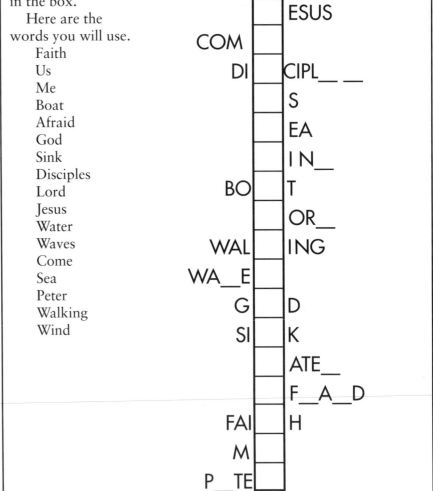

ESUS
COM◻
DI◻CIPL_ _
◻S
◻EA
◻IN_
BO◻T
◻OR_
WAL◻ING
WA__E◻
G◻D
SI◻K
◻ATE_
◻F_A_D
FAI◻H
M◻
P__TE◻

JESUS CALMED THE STORM

Scripture: **Mark 4:35-41**

Dot-to-Dot (Ages 3-6)

Connect the dots to finish this picture. Color the picture.

WHERE IS JESUS?

Scripture: **Mark 4:35-41**

Hidden Picture Puzzle (Ages 6-8)

Can you find Jesus in the storm? Color him.

WHAT HAPPENED?

Scripture: **Mark 4:35-41**

Criss-Cross Puzzle (Ages 8-12)

The names of important people from the New Testament are written below. They are written in a criss-cross pattern. Circle the letter where the names join together. Write the circled letters in the spaces below to decode the message found in the story.

__ __ __ __ __ __   __ __   __ __ __ __

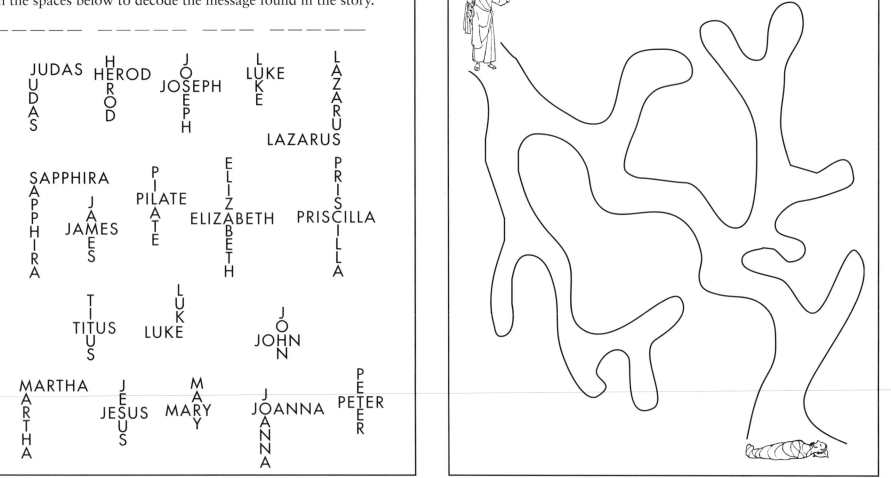

WHERE IS LAZARUS?

Scripture: **John 11:1-44**

Maze: (Ages 3-6)

Help Jesus find Lazarus. Draw a line from Jesus to Lazarus.

WHO DID JESUS RAISE FROM THE DEAD?

Scripture: John 11:1-44

Hidden Word Puzzle (Ages 6-8)

Jesus raised a friend from the dead. Follow the trail that connects letters to discover the friend's name. Write his name here. _____

WHAT DID JESUS SAY?

Scripture: John 11:1-44

Hidden Message (Ages 8-12)

See if you can find the name **Lazarus** hidden in the puzzle trail. Circle the letters of his name as you find them. (HINT: No two letters are side by side.) When you are finished, you will find some famous words spoken by Jesus.

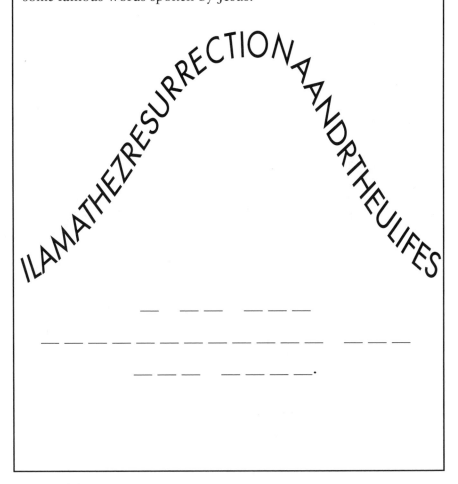

_ _ _ _ ___ ___

_____ ___ ___

___ ____.

WHAT DID JESUS RIDE?

Scripture: Matthew 21:1-11; Mark 11:1-11; Luke 19:28-40; John 12:12-19

Dot-to-Dot (Ages 3-6)

Can you connect the dots to make a picture of the animal that Jesus rode into Jerusalem? Color your picture.

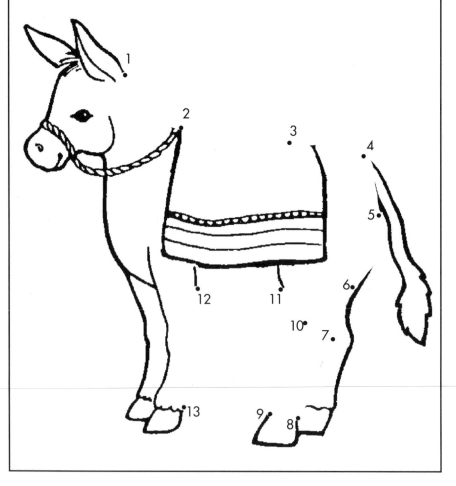

HELP US FIND THE WAY

Scripture: Matthew 21:1-11; Mark 11:1-11; Luke 19:28-40; John 12:12-19

Maze (Ages 6-8)

Can you help Jesus and the disciples find their way to Jerusalem?

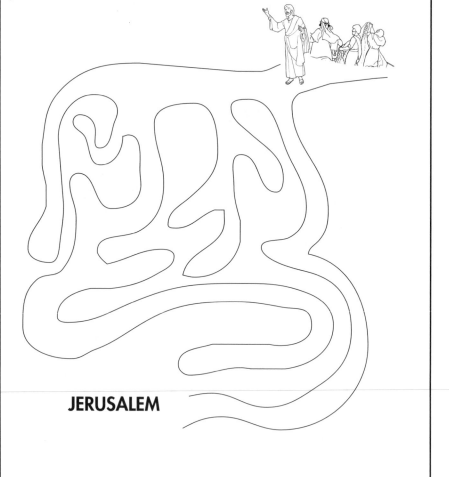

JERUSALEM

THE TRIUMPHAL ENTRY

Scripture: **Matthew 21:1-11; Mark 11:1-11; Luke 19:28-40; John 12:12-19**

Scrambled Words Puzzle (Ages 8-12)

Use your Bible to help you solve this puzzle. Look up each scripture listed to unscramble each word in the sentences. After you have found the correct words, write the letters that are circled. Unscramble that word to discover the "word of the day."

1. Jesus told the disciples to bring him a **(keydon)**
   _ ◯ ◯ _ _ _. (Matthew 21:1-2)

2. Jesus and his disciples were in **(thebgaphe)**
   _ _ _ ◯ _ _ ◯ _ _. (Matthew 21:1)

3. **(lebssed)** _ _ _ _ _ _ _ is the one who comes in the name of the Lord! (Matthew 21:9)

4. **(susej)** _ _ _ _ ◯ rode into Jerusalem on the donkey. (Matthew 21:7-10)

5. Jesus from **(zaraneth)** ◯ _ _ ◯ _ _ _ _.
   (Matthew 21:11)

   Write the letters that are circled. _____

   What word do they spell? _ _ _ _ _ _ _ _ _

   Why is this word special?

WHAT DID THEY EAT?

Scripture: **Matthew 26:17-30; Mark 14:12-26; Luke 22:7-30**

Dot-to-Dot (Ages 3-6)

Connect the dots to discover what Jesus and his disciples ate at the Last Supper.

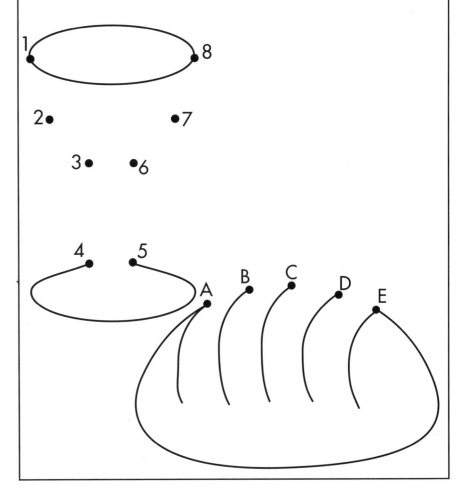

WHAT DID THEY EAT?

Scripture: Matthew 26:17-30; Mark 14:12-26; Luke 22:7-30

Hidden Pictures (Ages 6-8)

There are two items hidden in the picture. Find and color them. What are they? _____ and _____.
Why are they important? _____
_____
_____.

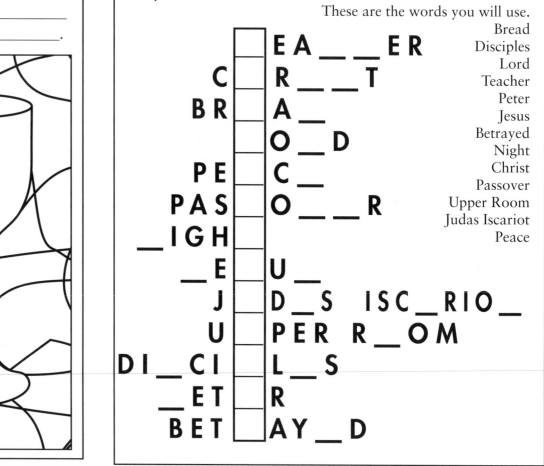

WHAT HAPPENED?

Scripture: Matthew 26:17-75; Mark 14:12-26; Luke 22:1-65

Word Puzzle (Ages 8-12)

Fill in the missing letters to spell an event that happened in the Bible. Look inside the box to discover the name of the event. Can you tell about it?

These are the words you will use.

Bread
Disciples
Lord
Teacher
Peter
Jesus
Betrayed
Night
Christ
Passover
Upper Room
Judas Iscariot
Peace

```
          E A _ _ _ E R
    C     R _ _ _ T
  B R     A _ _
          O _ _ D
  P E     C _ _
P A S     O _ _ _ R
_ I G H   |
  _ E     U _
    J     D _ S  I S C _ R I O _
    U     P E R  R _ O M
D I _ C I L _ S
  _ E T   R _
  B E T   A Y _ D
```

WHERE DID JESUS DIE?

Scripture: Matthew 27:1-61; Mark 15:1-47; Luke 23:1-56; John 18:28–19:42

Dot-to-Dot (Ages 3-6)

Connect the dots to make a picture of where Jesus died. Color your picture.

What is this a picture of?
Why is it special?

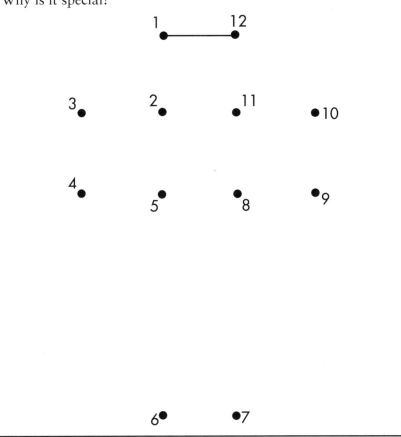

GOING TO CALVARY

Scripture: Matthew 27:1-61; Mark 15:1-47; Luke 23:1-56; John 18:28–19:42

Maze (Ages 6-8)

See if you can find the way to Calvary. Color your picture.

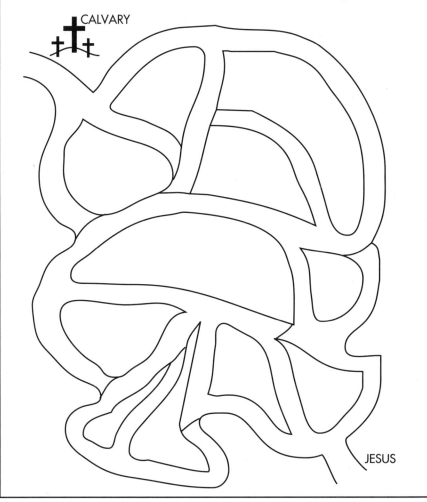

WHERE WERE THEY?

Scripture: **Matthew 27:1-61; Mark 15:1-47; Luke 23:1-56; John 18:28–19:42**

Criss-Cross (Ages 8-12)

Some important words about the Crucifixion are listed below. Circle the letters where each word joins. Write them in the spaces below to decode a message about the Crucifixion.

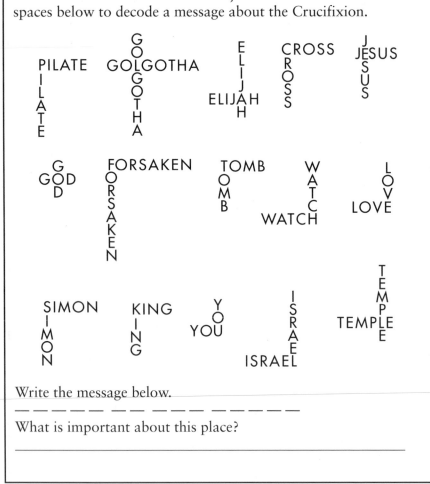

Write the message below.

_ _ _ _ _ _ _ _ _ _ _ _ _ _ _ _ _

What is important about this place?

_____

EASTER SUNDAY

Scripture: **Matthew 28; Mark 16; Luke 24; John 20–21**

Hidden Pictures (Ages 3-6)

Find and color these pictures.
Cross
Lily
What do they remind you of?

WHAT DID THEY SAY?

Scripture: **Matthew 28; Mark 16; Luke 24; John 20–21**

Shape Puzzle (Ages 6-8)

Color:
Hearts—Pink   Circles—Green   Triangles—Yellow

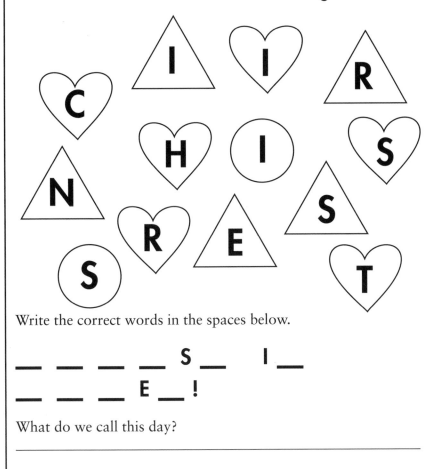

Write the correct words in the spaces below.

_ _ _ _ _ S _ I _

_ _ _ _ E _ !

What do we call this day?

_____

EASTER JOY

Scripture: **Matthew 28; Mark 16; Luke 24; John 20–21**

Word Search (Ages 8-12)

Draw a line through each word in the list as you find it in the puzzle. Words go across or down. When you have located all of the words, there will be some letters left over. Circle those letters to find the hidden word. They spell a word from the Bible story. (Hint: One word appears twice. Another clue goes in two directions!)

```
C L O V E G O O D F
S A V I O R J O Y R
M S B R E A D R A I
A T A O G Y S S N D
R S R J O O O P G A
Y U O D U N I E Y
G P S Y S K U L L T
O P E T E R R A N O
J E S U S M E T S M
C R U C I F I E D B
```

Last Supper	Good Friday	Savior	Crucified	God
Love	Peter	Pilate	Angel	Jesus
Joy	Us	Arose	You	Skull
Tomb	Bread	Mary	Ran	Son
Me	Go			

Word: _____

Why is this word special?_____

Which word appears twice? _____

Which clue goes in two directions? _____

GAMES FOR LEARNING BIBLE STORIES

Children enjoy playing games. Games help children learn and develop new skills. They are a good way to inspire children to learn Bible stories and lessons.

These games can be used as a way of breaking large groups into smaller groupings or as "icebreakers" to help children meet one another.

These games can be used in Sunday school and religious classrooms, Christian schools and day care programs, children's ministry events and intergenerational activities.

When playing these games, refrain from keeping score. Instead, play for the fun of playing and learning together.

Age level recommendations are provided for each game: ages 3-6 (preschool, kindergarten), ages 6-8 (grades 1-2), and ages 8-12 (grades 3-6).

 SOMETHING EXTRA

The activities in this section include stories and songs to enhance the lessons you teach with these games.

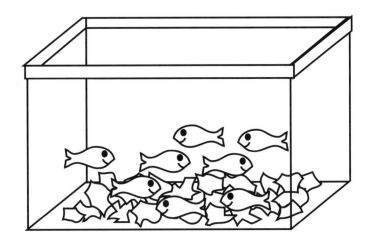

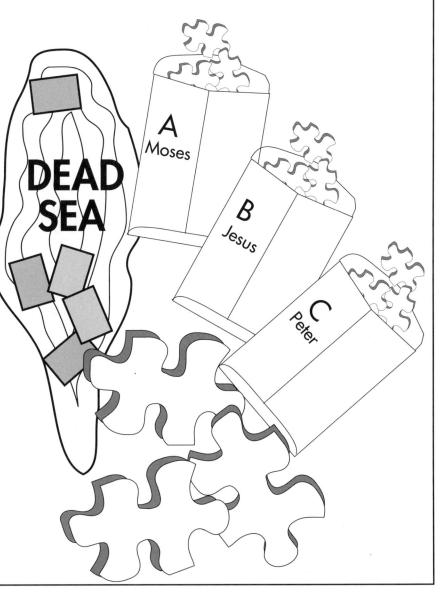

MISSING PIECES

Ages 3-12

Learning Goal: This activity gives children the opportunity to tell Bible stories in their own words.

✂ MATERIALS

Several jigsaw puzzles that depict a Bible story or biblical scene.
Felt-tip markers
One Bible per table
One table for each puzzle

HINT: To create your own puzzles, see Create a Puzzle on page 39.

PREPARATION

1. Label the outside of each puzzle box with a different letter of the alphabet.
2. Label the back of each puzzle piece with the letter that corresponds with the box it belongs to. (This ensures that all pieces from each puzzle stay together. It also helps children who are having difficulty locating the puzzle their piece belongs to.)
3. Place each puzzle on a separate table, and put each puzzle together.
4. Remove several pieces from each puzzle and place them in a paper bag.

➡ DIRECTIONS

1. As children arrive, let them choose a piece from the bag.
2. Tell the children to find the puzzle that their piece belongs to, fit the piece into the puzzle, and remain at that table.
3. After all puzzles have been completed, ask each group to tell the story the puzzle depicts. For older children ask: "Where in the Bible is the story found?" "What did you learn from the story?"

HINTS

1. If using this game with young children, use only two puzzles. Be prepared to offer assistance.
2. Older children and large groups of children can be challenged with more puzzles. If using the game with various age levels, encourage older children to help younger children.
3. This game can be easily adapted to work with different age groups and in various group settings.

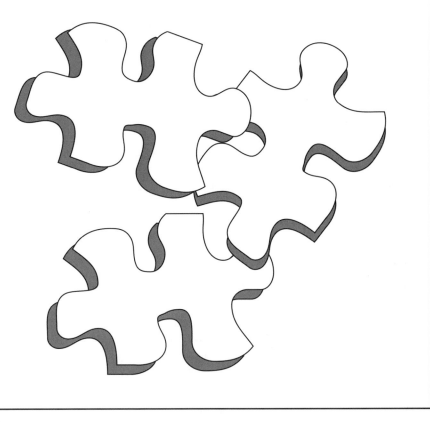

IT'S A PUZZLE

Ages 8-12

Learning Goal: Children will learn to tell Bible stories.

 **MATERIALS**

Several poster-sized pictures depicting biblical scenes, Bible stories, or biblical characters. (These can be ordered from religious materials suppliers.)
Permanent black fine-point marker
Large envelopes (10" x 13")
Clear contact paper (available in home, teacher, or art supply stores.)

PREPARATION

1. Cover both sides of each poster with clear contact paper.
2. Cut each poster into large puzzle pieces.
3. Label each envelope with the title of the poster and an alphabet letter.
4. Label the back of each poster piece with the corresponding letter.
5. Put all of the puzzle pieces into one bag prior to the children's arrival.

DIRECTIONS

1. Give each person a puzzle piece.
2. Instruct them to find others with pieces that match their puzzle.
3. When all of the groups have found one another and have completed putting their puzzles together, ask them to tell the story the poster illustrates, or to tell about the character pictured. Also, ask where the story or character is located in the Bible.
4. Discuss how that story affects us today.

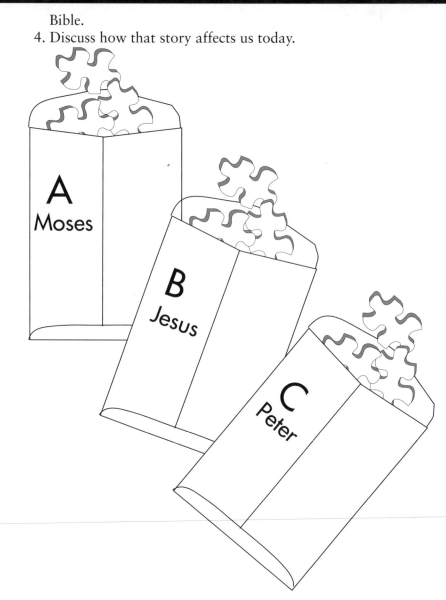

CREATE A PUZZLE

Ages 6-12

Learning Goal: Children will create their own puzzles based on Bible stories and characters.

MATERIALS

Crayons
Scissors
18" x 12" white cover stock paper (1 per person)
18" x 12" white construction paper (1 per person)
Pencils
10" x 13" envelopes (1 per person)
Permanent fine-point black marker
Clear contact paper
Rubber cement

DIRECTIONS

1. Ask each child to draw a picture of a scene that reminds them of something in the Bible (for example, a scene from a Bible story, a biblical character, a favorite verse). The picture can include words if desired.
2. Use rubber cement to glue the picture to a piece of cover stock paper.
3. Cover the picture with clear contact paper.
4. Cut the picture into large shapes to make a puzzle.
5. Give each child an envelope with a letter of the alphabet printed in one corner. Ask them to print the title of the puzzle and their name at the top. Next, label each puzzle piece with the appropriate alphabet letter.
6. Let the children work each other's puzzles.

IDEA

These puzzles can be used with the preceding games.

LESSON (USE WITH ANY OF THE PRECEDING PUZZLE ACTIVITIES.)

Talk about what happens when we try to fit the wrong pieces into a puzzle. Ask: "Why doesn't this work?"

Relate this to what happens when we try to do the wrong things in life. "Why doesn't it work to do wrong things? What happens when we do the wrong thing?"

Explain that life is puzzling. We have questions about the right way to do things. Sometimes we are tempted to do something wrong just to go along with what everyone else is doing. God has given us a book that helps us fit all of the pieces of life together in the right way. "What is that book?" (The Bible)

SOMETHING EXTRA

Share the story: *The Missing Piece* by Shel Silverstein

It was missing a piece. It looked and looked until it found its place, but things still weren't perfect.

Discuss this story: "How often do we search for something hoping it will make our lives perfect?" "What do we truly need to find?" Talk about following God. "How do we find what is important?" (Prayer asking God for help, and so forth)

BIBLE STORY WHEEL

Ages 3-12

Learning Goal: This activity helps children identify Bible characters and religious symbols.

✂ MATERIALS

Two round cardboard pizza trays (12" diameter)
Metal fasteners
Pictures that depict Bible stories, biblical characters or religious symbols (cross, manger, star, and so forth)
Clear contact paper
Tape
Scissors
Crayons

➡ DIRECTIONS

1. Cut a "pie slice" from one of the round pizza trays.
2. Cut out the Bible pictures and cover with clear contact. (If needed, color before covering with contact paper.)
3. Tape pictures along the outer edge of the cardboard tray that doesn't have the missing slice.
4. Make a hole in the center of the cardboard tray wheels and attach them using the fastener.
5. As you turn the wheel, a picture will appear through the opening.

♪ A SONG TO SING

Sing the first line and have the children repeat it.
Example:
  Teacher: Who is this?
  Children: Who is this?

WHO IS THIS? by Cindy Dingwall ("Frere Jacques")
  Who is this? Who is this?
  Can you guess? Can you guess?
  He had a coat of colors. He had a coat of colors.
  Who is this? Who is this?

WHAT IS THIS? by Cindy Dingwall ("Frere Jacques")
  What is this? What is this?
  Can you guess? Can you guess?
  It shined in the sky; it shined in the sky
  In Bethlehem. In Bethlehem.

Adapt the third line of the song to correspond with each Bible story, character, or symbol you used on the wheel, such as:
  Noah's Ark: "He built an ark of wood"
  Ten Commandments: "God gave him Ten Commandments
  Crucifixion: "Jesus died upon it"

After the song, let children tell who or what is pictured. Older children can tell why that person or symbol is important.
Use the Bible Story Wheel with any of the stories in this section.

❖ HINTS

1. Type the lyrics (words) to the song on an index card and tape it to the back of the wheel.
2. Make one wheel for each set of pictures you choose to use. Tape the appropriate set of lyrics to the back of each wheel. This allows you to have character, story, and symbol wheels.
3. To make interchangeable wheels, cover the bottom wheel with clear contact paper. Tape contact covered pictures of your choice to the bottom wheel. Tape appropriate lyrics to the back of the wheel and attach the top wheel. You can mix stories, characters, and symbols on one wheel. This method allows you to adapt the wheels to a variety of age levels.
4. Encourage older children to create the lyrics for the third line of the songs.

WHAT'S IN THE BAG?

Ages 3-12

Learning Goal: This activity helps children learn about the importance of Bible events, characters, and religious symbols.

 MATERIALS

Attractive gift bag (Try to find one with a religious theme.) Objects that represent Bible stories, events, biblical characters, or religious symbols. (Pictures can be used but objects are more effective.)

 **PREPARATION**

Put the objects into the bag.

▶ **DIRECTIONS**

1. Hold the bag so no one can see inside. Invite each child to pull something out of the bag and show it to the group. Ask: "What Bible story does this depict? Can you tell about it?"
2. If religious symbols (for example, candy cane, candle, wreath), are used, ask the children to explain the meaning of each one.
3. If characters are used, ask the students to tell who they are and something about them.

HINTS

1. Provide younger children with hints. (For example, Manger— What was the name of the baby who slept in a manger in Bethlehem?)
2. To challenge older children, blindfold them and ask them to feel an object and guess what it is. Ask them to tell something about it.

MATCH MAKERS

Ages 8-12

Learning Goal: This activity helps children learn to match the beginning and ending of Bible verses.

MATERIALS

Index cards in two colors (for example, yellow, green)
Black felt pens

PREPARATION

1. Choose a variety of Bible verses.
2. On the green cards neatly print the *first half* of each Bible verse selected.
3. On the yellow cards neatly print the *second half* of each Bible verse selected.

DIRECTIONS

1. Give each person a green card or a yellow card.
2. Tell the players to find the person with the other half of their Bible verse.
3. When everyone is matched, ask them to name the book, chapter, and verse where the scripture is found.

HINT

Make a master list of all the verses used including the book, chapter, and verse.

IDEA

This game works exceptionally well with "The Beatitudes."

But when the discipes saw him walking on the sea, they were terrified.

for it is such as these that the kingdom of heaven belongs."

Jesus said, "Let the little children come to me, and do not stop them;

Jesus spoke to them and said, "Take

But many who are first will be last,

and the last will be first.

PRAISE GOD!

Ages 8-12

Learning Goal: This activity helps children learn Bible verses.

MATERIALS

Set of green and yellow cards from the "Match Makers" game found on page 42

DIRECTIONS

Option 1

Deal five green cards to each person. The leader chooses a yellow card and reads it. The person holding the corresponding green card says, "Praise God!" and is given the yellow card. When all of the cards are matched, have each person read one of the verses on the cards. If they can identify book, chapter, and verse, they keep their cards. If not, whoever can identify book, chapter, and verse wins that set of cards. Have the group shout, "Praise God!" as a child wins a set of cards.

Option 2

Play until all the verses have been identified. If there are some that are difficult to identify, use a concordance and a Bible to look them up. Ask the students to read the verses aloud. Discuss the meaning of the verses and how they can be applied to our lives today.

But when the disciples saw him walking on the sea, they were terrified.

Jesus said, "Let the little children come to me, and do not stop them;

But many who are first will be last,

A PICTURE IS WORTH

Ages 6-12

Learning Goal: Children will identify Bible verses and stories using pictures and one-word clues.

✂ MATERIALS

Index cards
Black felt pens

 PREPARATION

Prior to class prepare a set of index cards with pictures and one-word clues. See the following ideas.

➡ DIRECTIONS

1. Give each child a card.
2. Ask the children to identify the story it depicts, give the book, chapter, and verse it is from, tell the entire story.
3. Ask the children if they can tell what each verse means.

💡 IDEA

Use this game to highlight Bible stories included in this book or to teach a specific Bible verse.

IDEAS FOR "A PICTURE IS WORTH"

Noah's Ark
▲ Genesis 6–9

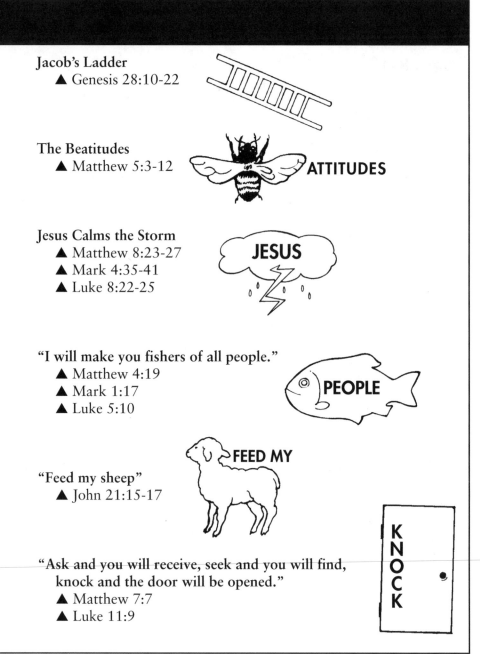

Jacob's Ladder
▲ Genesis 28:10-22

The Beatitudes
▲ Matthew 5:3-12

Jesus Calms the Storm
▲ Matthew 8:23-27
▲ Mark 4:35-41
▲ Luke 8:22-25

"I will make you fishers of all people."
▲ Matthew 4:19
▲ Mark 1:17
▲ Luke 5:10

"Feed my sheep"
▲ John 21:15-17

"Ask and you will receive, seek and you will find, knock and the door will be opened."
▲ Matthew 7:7
▲ Luke 11:9

ALLELUIA!

Ages 8-12

Learning Goal: This activity will help children learn and remember Bible verses.

 **MATERIALS**

Make a set of cards containing ideas from the *Match Makers* game on page 42, and *A Picture is Worth* game on page 44.
"The Dead Sea"—a large piece of brown paper cut in the shape of the Dead Sea.

DIRECTIONS

1. Place the Dead Sea on a table.
2. Lay the cards face down on the table.
3. Let each person have a turn taking a card.
4. If a scripture card is selected, ask the student to fill in the missing portion of the scripture and tell the book, chapter, and verse where it is found.
5. If a picture/word card is chosen, the student must briefly summarize the story as well as tell book, chapter, verse.
6. Those giving correct answers may keep the cards. If an incorrect answer is given, another player may try to answer. If that person answers correctly, he or she keeps the card. If no one knows the correct answer, it goes into *The Dead Sea*. Shout "Alleluia!" for correct responses.
7. After all of the cards have been used, take the ones from the "Dead Sea" and, using a concordance, look them up in the Bible. When the answer is found, shout "Alleluia!"

 **HINT**

Make a master list that includes the Bible references.

TREASURE HUNT

Ages 6-12

Learning Goal: This activity allows children to tell Bible stories using props.

MATERIALS

Objects depicting a variety of Bible stories
One paper bag per team
One Bible per team

PREPARATION

1. Select five (more or less depending on size of the class or group) Bible stories. Select stories that allow you to locate objects to represent them.
2. Prepare one bag per team. Write the name of the story and where it is found in the Bible. On the outside of the bag, list the objects that must be found.
3. Hide the objects.

➡️ DIRECTIONS

1. Divide the children into teams of two to four players.
2. Give each team a paper bag and a Bible. Have the teams find and read the story listed on the bag.
3. As any object is found, it should be placed in the bag.
4. When all objects have been found, each group takes a turn telling their story using the objects in their bag as props.

STORY IDEAS FOR TREASURE HUNT

Story: *Creation* (Genesis 1–2:3)
Objects: tree, flower, snowflake, person (doll), animals (plastic or stuffed)

Story: *Noah's Ark:* (Genesis 6–9)
Objects: ark, 2 identical plastic animals, cloud, rainbow, dove

Story: *Birth of Christ:* (Matthew 1:18–2:12, Luke 2:1-20)
Objects: star, manger with Jesus, donkey, angel, shepherd

Story: *Jesus Feeds Five Thousand:* (Matthew 14:15-21, Mark 6:35-44, Luke 9:12-17, John 6:5-14)
Objects: two fish, five loaves of bread, picture of thousands of people, Jesus statue, basket

HINTS

1. If you are playing with a mixed age group, try to pair an older child with a younger child (six-year-old with a nine-year-old; seven-year-old with a ten-year-old). Ask the older children to help with reading.
2. If possible, hide each group's object in a different room. This eliminates the problem of one group accidentally finding another group's objects.

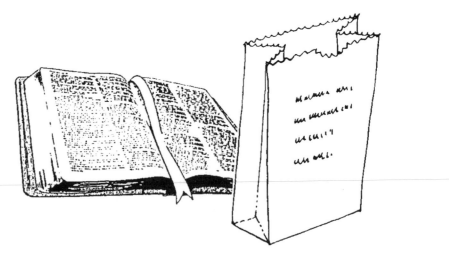

FROM THE BEGINNING PLEASE

Ages 8-12

Learning Goal: This activity helps children learn the psalms, stories, and prayers found in the Bible.

MATERIALS

Different colored index cards
Felt pens

PREPARATION

Choose different colored cards for each story, psalm or prayer. Write one verse of the story, psalm or prayer on each card.

DIRECTIONS

1. Divide the children into groups.
2. Give each person an index card with a verse on it. Have each group put themselves in the proper order, so the scripture reads correctly.
3. When it is time for each group to present their scripture, say, "From the beginning, please," and then each person reads what is on his or her card. For more of a challenge, see if the children can recite the story or psalm as a group.
4. For a large group use several different scriptures (for example, Lord's Prayer, Beatitudes, Ten Commandments). Have the children find their other group mates and arrange themselves in the proper order. As you call on each group to share say, "From the beginning, please."

Scripture Ideas: Ten Commandments, Psalms, Beatitudes, Lord's Prayer

VARIATION

Try this game with songs and hymns. After people are in the correct order, they must sing the songs or hymns.

HINT

Make a master list that tells what order each story, psalm or prayer comes in. Note the color you used for each type.

Ages 8-12

Learning Goal: Children will become acquainted with the books of the Bible and begin to learn about each book.

 **MATERIALS**

Different colored index cards
Felt pens
Bibles (one per person)
Pencils (one per person)
Lined notebook paper (one sheet per person)
One table per group and one chair per person

 PREPARATION

1. Label each table with a book of the Bible.
2. Choose several biblical books you wish to highlight.
3. Choose a color for each book. Write one letter of the title of a book on a card (for example, pink = "G" for Genesis).
4. Scramble the cards.

DIRECTIONS

1. Give each person an index card with a letter written on it.
2. Instruct children to find the others who have the remaining letters that spell out the title of their book of the Bible.
3. Have each group sit at the correct table.
4. Instruct each person to open their Bible to the book their group is working on and skim through that book to find names, places, events, and so forth that begin with the letter on their card.
5. Can they tell the significance of the words they located? If not, explain the words to them.

Examples:
G God, Garden
E Earth, Eden, Eve
N Night, Noah
E Eat, Esau, Egypt   L Levi, Lazarus
S Sodom, Simeon   U Upper Room
I Isaac, Ishmael   K King, Kingdom, Knock
S Snake, Stars   E Elizabeth, Enemies

HINT

Do some detective work beforehand. Make sure all of the letters in the books you select can be found. Have children work with the same translation (NIV, NRSV, and so forth).

SPIN 'N' TELL

Ages 3-8

Learning Goal: Children will identify and tell about Bible characters and symbols.

✂ MATERIALS

Several round (12" diameter) cardboard pizza trays
Spinners and brackets (available in teacher stores and office supply stores)
Glue
Pictures of biblical symbols and characters from coloring books, flannel board pattern books, Bible clip art books
Crayons
Clear contact paper

PREPARATION

1. Create several disks (one with Bible characters, one with Bible symbols, and so forth)
2. Divide the disks into 4 to 8 segments
3. Choose the pictures you want on each disk
4. Copy, color, and cut out each picture
5. Glue a picture to each one of the disk segments
6. Cover the disk with clear contact paper
7. Use bracket to attach the spinner in the center of disk

➡ DIRECTIONS

Let children take turns spinning the spinner. When the spinner lands on a picture, children must tell who or what it is and a little about it.

HINTS:

▲ Vary difficulty of the game with age and ability of children.
▲ Very young children (ages 3-6) can tell what the picture is. The adult can help them tell a little more about it.
▲ Use the disk with four segments with younger children (ages 3-6).
▲ Older children (ages 7-8) can identify the picture and tell about the character, summarize the story, or tell what the symbol means.
▲ Use the eight-segment disk with older children (ages 7-8).

LET'S GO FISHING

Ages 3-8

Learning Goal: This activity helps children learn about being "fishers of people."

MATERIALS

Camera and film
One paper cut-out fish per child. See Appendix page 178. (use a variety of colors)

Fish pond
    Large box
    Blue plastic food wrap
    Blue tissue paper
    Clear, heavy book tape

Fishing rod
    Dowel rod
    Long piece of narrow rope
    Paper clips
    Magnet

Large needle strung with one yard of colorful yarn.
Sign that reads, "Look Who Jesus Caught for Followers."
Rubber cement or glue
Paper punch
Marker

PREPARATION

1. A week before you plan to use this game take a photo of each child. Cut each photo into a circle.
2. Make the fish pond from the box. Cut one lengthwise side of the box off. Place the blue food wrap across the opening attaching it with heavy book tape. Bunch up the blue tissue paper and place it inside the box.
3. Attach the children's pictures with their names to a fish. Attach paper clips to the fish. Put the fish (picture side down) on top of the blue tissue.
4. Tie a piece of rope to a dowel rod to make a fishing rod. Attach the magnet to the end of the rope with glue.

DIRECTIONS

1. Let each child take a turn at being "Jesus."
2. Drop the string into the pond and try to catch a fish.
3. When "Jesus" snares a fish, he or she can pull it up to see who has been caught.
4. The child who was caught becomes the next "Jesus."
5. As the fish with the children's photos are caught, string them onto the yarn with the needle. When all of the fish have been caught, hang the "fish" where everyone can see them. Place the sign nearby.
6. This makes an eye-catching display inside your classroom or right by the door outside the classroom.

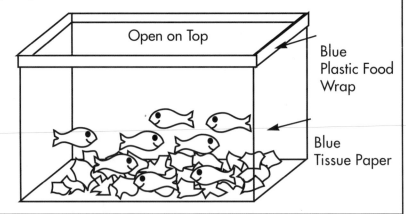

VARIATIONS OF WELL-KNOWN GAMES

Pin the Tail on the Donkey (Ages 3-8)

▲ Put the sun in the sky (Creation)
▲ Put Noah on the Ark (Noah's Ark)
▲ Put the angels on the ladder (Jacob's Ladder)
▲ Put the coat on Joseph (Joseph & the Coat of Many Colors)
▲ Put the tablets in Moses' hands (10 Commandments)
▲ Put Jonah inside the whale (Jonah and the Whale)
▲ Put Jesus in the Manger/Put the star in the sky (Birth of Christ)
▲ Put Jesus on the Mountain (Sermon on the Mount)
▲ Put Jesus/Peter on the water (Jesus Walks on Water)
▲ Put Jesus on the donkey (Palm Sunday)

Simon Says (Ages 3-8)

▲ Substitute "Jesus Says"
▲ For older children: Have Jesus give commands that he would give: "Smile at a friend." "Wave hello."
▲ The Devil says: "Make a mean face." "Hit someone." Discuss whether these actions are right or wrong and why.

Mother May I? (Ages 6-8)

▲ Substitute "Jesus May I?"
▲ Have two children stand facing the group. Have the rest of the group form a straight line across the area facing the two kids.
▲ The child on the left will give commands. The child on the right is Jesus (let girls have the opportunity to be Jesus as well as boys)

Child giving command:	*Jason take three tiny steps forward.*
Jason:	*Jesus, may I?*
Jesus:	*Yes, you may, Jason.*
Child giving command:	*Lisa, hit Tommy.*
Lisa:	*Jesus, may I?*
Jesus:	*No, Lisa!*
Lisa:	*Why not?*
Jesus:	*Because hitting hurts and it isn't kind to hit and hurt people.*

Continue to play in this fashion until all children have joined Jesus. When all children have joined Jesus everybody can yell "PRAISE THE LORD!"

BIBLE ART

The projects in the section may be used with various Bible stories or scripture passages. They allow children to use their creativity and imagination as they design projects that highlight Bible stories and lessons.

They can be used in Sunday school programs, Vacation Bible School, children's ministry events, Christian day care, and school classrooms.

Age recommendations are provided for each project: ages 3-6 (preschool, kindergarten), ages 6-8 (grades 1 and 2), and ages 8-12 (grades 3-6).

Additional art projects that accompany individual stories are in the section titled "Presenting Bible Stories" on pages 67–115.

The activities in this section use a variety of art materials. Use the following checklist to keep materials readily available for teachers and children.

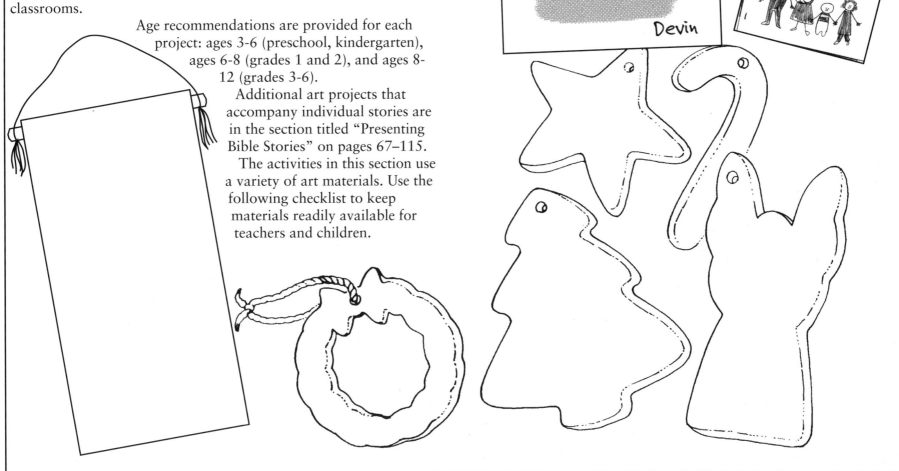

ART MATERIALS CHECKLIST

- ❏ Powdered tempera paints in as many colors as possible. One jar lasts a long time and using powdered paints allows you to mix colors easily and to vary the thickness of the paints.
- ❏ Paint brushes
- ❏ Crayons
- ❏ Scissors
- ❏ Glue sticks
- ❏ Bottled glue (individual bottles)
- ❏ Glue gun with glue (teacher use only)
- ❏ Pencils
- ❏ Colored pencils
- ❏ Colored markers
- ❏ Waterproof black markers
- ❏ Yarn in a variety of colors
- ❏ Dowel rods
- ❏ Felt in a variety of colors
- ❏ Pellon nonwoven textile
- ❏ Scraps of fabric (in a variety of colors, prints, and textures)
- ❏ Envelopes

- ❏ Colored construction paper (9" x 12" and 12" x 18")
- ❏ White construction paper (9" x 12" and 12" x 18")
- ❏ Cover stock paper (9" x 12" and 12" x 18")
- ❏ Newspapers (for covering work areas)
- ❏ Glitter, sequins
- ❏ Flannel Board pattern books
- ❏ Coloring books (for patterns)
- ❏ Cookie cutters (Christmas, Easter, and other religious symbols)
- ❏ Plywood
- ❏ Decoupage solution
- ❏ Plastic nonflexible drinking straws
- ❏ Metal picture hangers
- ❏ Wooden stain spray paint
- ❏ Needles and thread
- ❏ Soup cans
- ❏ Meat packing trays
- ❏ Ribbons (variety of colors, patterns, widths)
- ❏ Other items:

TRASH TO TREASURES BOX

Ask your congregation to fill this box with art materials you can use for projects. Put a large box in an easy to access place in your church with a big sign that reads: *Trash to Treasures Box*. Provide a list of materials you need in the church or parent newsletter and/or inserted into the church bulletin. Provide reminders about this box during announcements as well. Also, beside your box, provide copies of the lists so people can take them home.

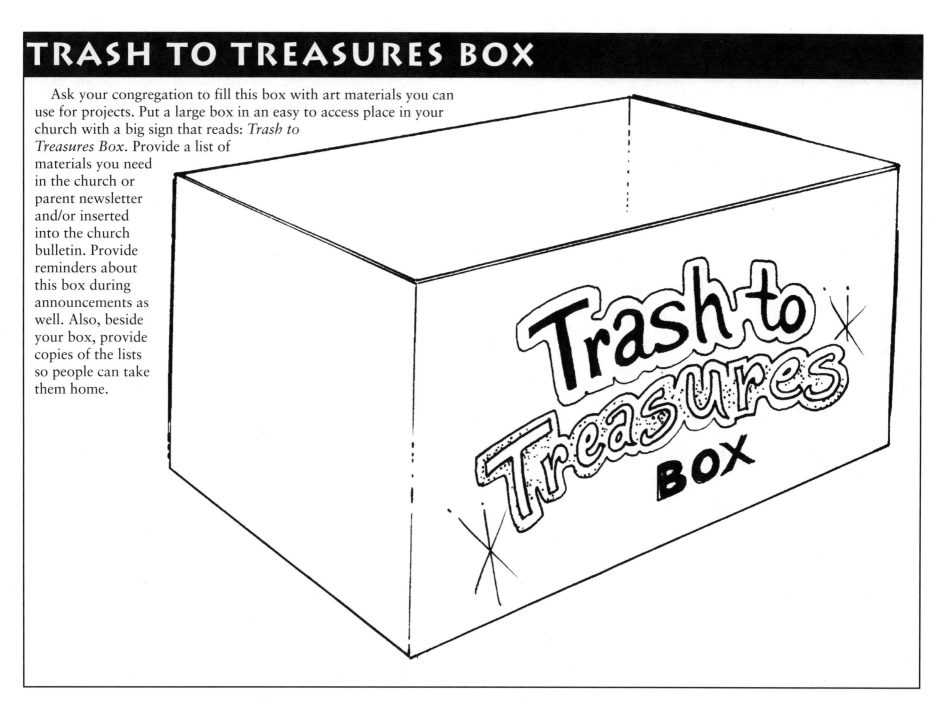

BIBLE BANNERS

Ages 3-12

Learning Goal: The banners highlight a Bible story, verse or psalm.

✂ MATERIALS

One piece of colored felt (2' x 1' or 3' x 2') per person
Pieces of felt cut into shapes representing Bible stories, psalms or verses (one packet of these per child). You may also use pieces of fabric and materials with different textures if desired.
One piece of yarn (cut into 1-yard lengths) per person
Glue (one bottle per person)
Glue gun and glue sticks or sewing machine
1 dowel rod ¼" diameter by 14" long or ¼" diameter by 28" long per person
Envelopes for storing shapes
Marker
White piece of felt with the title of the story, the psalm or Bible verse written with permanent black marker (one per child)

PREPARATION

1. Choose a story, psalm or Bible verse to highlight.
2. Stitch or glue (using glue gun) the top edge (2-3 inches) of the felt down. If gluing, allow 24 hours drying time before continuing work on the banner.
3. Put each child's shapes into a separate envelope.

➡ DIRECTIONS

Discuss the story, psalm or Bible verse you will highlight with your banner. Give each child a banner and an envelope containing the shapes they will use. Allow children to arrange the shapes on their banners. Glue the shapes into place. Slip the dowel rod through the slot at the top and attach the yarn so the banner can be hung. Print the child's name in the lower left corner of the banner. Hang the banners in the classroom or church. After a few weeks let the children take their banners home.

BANNER MURALS

Ages 3-12

Learning Goal: This activity helps children tell a Bible story through pictures.

✂ MATERIALS

One piece of light gray or blue colored felt 6' x 2'.
Fabric rope to use in hanging banner mural
Precut felt and Pellon figures that illustrate a Bible story
Flannel board pattern books
Crayons
Fabric paints
Glitter
Glue or Needle and thread
Batting (for clouds)
12" colored ribbons (10 ribbons in 5 colors)
Dowel rod for hanging banner
Straight pins with colored heads

PREPARATION

Stitch or glue (with glue gun) down a 2" seam along the top of the long piece of felt, where the dowel rod will be slipped through.

➡ DIRECTIONS

1. Each child is responsible for one portion of the story. Have each child color their felt/Pellon pieces. Arrange and pin the background (clouds, hills, grass, and so forth). Add the rest of the figures so that the story is told in proper order moving from left to right. Pin these to the felt. Glue or hand stitch the pieces to the mural. (Pellon works better sewn than glued.)

2. Insert the dowel rod through the top. Attach the colored ribbon to the ends of the rod. Attach the rope to the rod for hanging. Place the banner mural on permanent display. Hang an attractive sign listing the names of the creators of the banner mural beside the mural, with a photo of the group.

3. Honor everyone who worked on the mural at a dedication ceremony during the worship service or a special program.

🧩 HINT

This project makes a good vacation Bible school or summer Sundays project, because the steps can take several days or weeks to complete.

PSALM PLAQUES

Ages 8-12

Learning Goal: Each child will create a plaque that highlights a psalm.

✂ MATERIALS

9" x 11" piece of white cover stock paper (one per person)
2 clean paint brushes per color
Individual cups of water (use empty margarine tubs—one for each color)
Tempera paints in pastel colors (yellow, peach, pink, lavender, blue, green)—put in margarine tubs, tin cans, or frosting tubs)
Pencils
Permanent black felt markers
Measuring spoons
1 6"-piece of yarn per person
Scissors
Clear book tape

PREPARATION

1. Choose several short psalms (or portions of psalms) from the Bible such as: *Psalm 23; Psalm 46:1; Psalm 100; Psalm 118:1; Psalm 118:24; Psalm 121; Psalm 124:8; Psalm 135:3; Psalm 146:2, or Psalm 150.*
2. Using a pencil draw faint lines on each piece of white paper.
3. Mix pastel paints. Begin with white tempera and mix well with water. Use a measuring spoon to add a very small amount of colored tempera to the white paint. Keep the mixture thin and watery in texture.
4. Mark paint brushes with a swatch of the paint color to be used. This will keep the brushes from getting mixed up. These swatches can be washed off when finished.

▶ DIRECTIONS

1. Choose a psalm or verse. Use a pencil to copy the text including the scripture onto the white paper, using the lines as guides. Print lightly. Write your name in small letters at the bottom of the paper. Trace over the writing with permanent black marker. Allow five minutes to dry. Carefully erase any visible pencil lines.
2. Choose a color(s) to brush across the paper. Dip paint brush into the tub of water first, then into the paint tub, and then onto the paper. Let the paintings dry overnight. Tie a piece of yarn into a loop for hanging and securely tape it to the back with book tape.

✦ HINTS

1. If some children find writing difficult, print the psalm for them. If necessary, also go over it with marker. Let the child do the actual painting.
2. These plaques make nice Mother's or Father's Day gifts.

✕ VARIATION

Optional:
Wooden plaques
Decoupage solution
Decorative ribbon
Metal picture hangers
Wood stain (spray)
Paint brushes (for decoupage)
Mount psalms onto wooden plaques. You will need one piece of plywood per child (10" x 12"). Stain the plaques with a wood grain stain several days before class. Attach a metal picture hanger to the back. Let pictures dry overnight. Laminate or cover both sides with clear Contact paper. Use decoupage solution to mount picture on the plaque. Use decorate ribbon to make an edging around the paper.

SCRIPTURE PICTURES

Ages 8-12

Learning Goal: Each child will design a project that highlights one or two verses of scripture.

MATERIALS

1 piece of heavy white construction paper (9" x 11") (one per person)
1 piece of heavy colored construction paper (10" x 12") (one per person)
Pencils
Tempera paints (green, yellow, orange, red, blue)
Paint brushes (2 per color)—mark each brush with paint swatch
Margarine tubs for water
Permanent black markers
Rubber cement
Book tape
     1 6" piece of yarn per person

PREPARATION

1. Select a variety of easy-to-read scripture verses (for example, Matthew 7:7; Matthew 11:28; Matthew 18:20; John 6:20; Romans 8:28; Philippians 4:7; Philippians 4:13; 1 John 4:1).
2. Place paper in horizontal position, and use a ruler and pencil to lightly draw several lines across the paper leaving even margins on all four sides.
3. Fold paper vertically in half leaving a light crease through the center. Open paper.

DIRECTIONS

1. Choose a scripture. Using a pencil, lightly write the scripture onto the lines on the paper. Trace the writing with permanent marker. Write your name in the lower left corner. Allow 5 minutes to dry.
2. Choose two colors of paint (Good combinations are: green/yellow; orange/yellow; orange/red; red/yellow; blue/red; blue/green)
3. Use the paint brushes to dab one color along each side of the fold (for example, green on left, yellow on right). Be careful not to mix the colors. Be sure to just dab the paint on the paper. *Avoid* making brush strokes or painting over the writing.
4. Fold the left side over onto the right side and lightly rub with the palm of your hand. Open the paper carefully to see the completed design. Let dry overnight. Use rubber cement to mount the pictures onto the larger piece of construction paper. Make a loop with the yarn and attach it to the back of the picture with book tape.

HINTS

1. A child who has difficulty writing may need help copying a verse.
2. These pictures make nice gifts for parents.

VARIATION

The pictures can also be mounted. See page 58.

PRAYERFUL THOUGHTS

Ages 3-12

Learning Goal: Each child will create a prayer that thanks God.

 **MATERIALS**

8" x 10" white construction paper (one per child)
9" x 11" colored cover stock paper (one per child)
Tempera paints
Sponges (purchase different shapes or cut your own into one-inch squares)
Permanent felt tip markers (one per person)
   (Suggested colors: red, green, blue, purple)
Margarine tubs (one per color)
Several pages of newspaper
Rubber cement

 PREPARATION

Mix tempera paints so they are thick in consistency.

➡ DIRECTIONS

1. Ask everyone to complete this sentence: "I give thanks to God for . . ." Use a pencil to print the entire sentence onto the white construction paper. Trace the words with a colored marker. When dry, carefully erase visible pencil lines.
2. Choose a sponge shape. Dip the sponge in one color of paint.
3. Lightly press the sponge on the paper, so you can see the shape. *Avoid* rubbing or stroking with the sponge. Allow to dry for 24 hours. Mount the prayers onto the cover stock paper using rubber cement. Tie a piece of yarn into loop and attach it to the back with book tape.

 HINT

Only dip a sponge in one color. You will need to write the sentence for younger children or those who find writing difficult. Allow children to do the painting.

 **VARIATION**

To mount the prayers onto wood, see page 58.

Ages 6-12

Learning Goal: This activity highlights a favorite Bible verse.

 **MATERIALS**

White typing paper (2 sheets per person)
Paint brushes (2 per color)
1 pencil per person
Black felt markers (one per person)
Tempera paints
Margarine tubs with water and paints
1 white crayon per person
9" x 12" colored cover stock paper (one per person)

 PREPARATION

1. Select several short Bible verses. Print them on a sheet of paper to make it easier for the children to copy them.
2. Mix tempera paints into the margarine tubs. Keep the mixture very watery.
3. Provide additional margarine tubs filled with water.
4. Use pencils to lightly draw lines onto typing paper (one sheet per person).

→ DIRECTIONS

1. Choose a verse. Use pencil to write the verse onto a sheet of white paper with lines. Trace with black marker.
2. Lay the second sheet of paper on top of the first sheet of paper. Use the white crayon to trace the verse onto the top piece of paper, pressing firmly. (An adult may need to go over white lines.) Select a paint color. Dip the paint brush into the water and then into the paint. Lightly brush the paint across the paper. Cover the entire paper with paint. The white letters will show through the paint.
3. Allow the pictures to dry overnight. Use rubber cement to mount the pictures onto cover stock paper. Use felt marker to write your name in the bottom left corner.

 **HINT**

Children who have difficulty writing may need assistance.

 **VARIATION**

To mount the pictures onto wooden plaques, see page 58.

OUR PRAYER

Ages 3-12

Learning Goal: Children will create a prayer that they can use at home with their families, in a Sunday school class, or during the worship service.

MATERIALS

8" x 10" pieces of white construction paper (one per person)
9" x 11" pieces of colored cover stock paper (one per person)
1 plastic nonflexible drinking straw per person
Tempera paints (blue, green, orange, red, yellow, purple)
2 paint brushes per color
Margarine tubs for paints
Rubber cement
Six-inch pieces of yarn (one per person)
Black felt tip marker

PREPARATION

Use margarine tubs to mix tempera paints. Make them watery.

DIRECTIONS

1. Compose a group prayer. Example: "Thank you God for . . . " "Allow each child to supply a one- or two-word ending. List all of the endings to complete the prayer.
2. Print the completed prayer onto typing paper and make one copy per child. With a paint brush drop paint onto the paper. Use straw to blow the paint around, being careful not to touch the paint with your straw or hands. Repeat this process with several colors.

HINT

Make extra copies of the prayer in case printing accidents occur. Practice *blowing* through the straw before you begin.
After the pictures dry, use a marker to print each child's name in the lower, left corner. Use rubber cement to mount the pictures onto the cover stock paper. Make a loop with yarn, and attach it to the back of the prayer with book tape.

These make nice gifts for parents.

VARIATION

To mount the prayers onto wooden plaques, see page 58.

Thank you God for...
My mommy and daddy.
My teacher
My puppy

Sean

GOD IS . . .

Ages 3-12

Learning Goal: Children will think about all that God is to them.

MATERIALS

9" x 12" pieces of color cover stock paper (one per child)
Powdered tempera paints (blue, green, orange, red, purple)
Cotton balls (1 per color for each child)
Margarine tubs
Large spoon
Hair spray
Rubber cement
Typing or copy paper
Black felt tip pen

PREPARATION

Put one large spoonful of dry tempera without water into each tub

DIRECTIONS

1. Think of words to describe God (for example, my friend, my companion, loving, kind, helpful, my creator, caring, awesome, wonderful, good, and so forth).
2. Compose a group prayer using all of the adjectives.
   Example: God is my friend and my companion.
            God is wonderful. God is my helper.
            God is awesome and good. God is loving and caring.
            God is my creator. AMEN.
3. Use felt pen to neatly print this prayer on a piece of white typing paper. Make one copy per child, plus a few extras. Dip cotton balls into the powdered tempera and brush them across the paper. With black marker, print the child's name in the lower left corner. Spray the picture with hair spray to set the tempera.

HINTS

1. Spray the pictures outdoors since many people are allergic to aerosol sprays.
2. Use rubber cement to mount these onto cover stock paper.

VARIATION

If you prefer to mount these onto wooden plaques, see page 58.

GOD SHOWS LOVE FOR US BY

Ages 3-12

Learning Goal: Children will be encouraged to think about how God shows us love and will create a book for the church library or for a sick or hospitalized child.

✂ MATERIALS

8" x 10" pieces of white construction paper (one per child)
Crayons
Black felt markers
Staples or brackets
Clear Contact paper
Paper punch

➡ DIRECTIONS

1. Create a book titled "God Shows Love for Us by . . ."
2. Each person will make one page of the book.
3. Think about ways God shows us love (for example, giving us food to eat, creating flowers, and so forth). Say: Draw a picture of how God shows love for your page of the book.
4. Compose an ending to the sentence, "God shows love for us by . . ." and write it on your paper.
5. Let one child create an attractive cover for the book. Write the title *God Shows Love for Us* on the cover. Add **Written by:** (list class, group, and so forth).
6. Use clear Contact paper to protect the front and back cover. Staple the book together. If the book is too thick, punch three holes along the left side and fasten with brackets.

✾ HINTS

1. This project works best if the pages are horizontal rather than vertical.
2. Help children with printing as needed.

CHRISTMAS SYMBOL ORNAMENTS

Ages 3-12

Learning Goal: Each child will create several ornaments that will help them learn about Christmas symbols.

✂ MATERIALS

Play dough (red, green, white)
Cookie cutters in a variety of Christmas shapes
    (tree, wreath, candy cane, star, and so forth)
Pencils
Red and green powdered tempera
Yarn
Glitter in a variety of colors (red, green, gold, silver, multicolor)
Rolling pin
Several pieces of tissue paper per child
Paper lunch sacks (one per child)
White, self-stick labels
Glue
Large margarine tubs

 PREPARATION

Play Dough Recipe
1 cup flour
1 cup salt
½ cup water
1. Mix flour and salt together. Add water slowly, mixing as you add it. Mix until dough is firm but pliable. It should not be flaky or gooey. Add additional flour or water to make dough the proper consistency. Have both available in the room as you work.

2. Make several batches of dough. Add a small amount of powdered red tempera to one batch and green to another batch. Leave one batch white. Store the play dough in large empty margarine tubs rather than plastic bags.

▶ DIRECTIONS

1. Roll play dough so it is about ⅛ inch thick.
2. Talk about the significance of each of the Christmas symbols.
3. Use cookie cutters to cut shapes from the play dough. Set dough shapes on a cookie sheet. (Make note of where each child's shapes are located.)
4. Use a pencil eraser to poke a hole in the top of each ornament.
5. Bake ornaments at 325 degrees for about 15 minutes or until dry and hard. Let cool. Decorate the ornaments with glitter. Loop a piece of yarn through each ornament. Tie ends of yarn together.
6. Wrap each ornament in tissue paper. Attach a label that tells who the gift is for and who it is from. Place ornaments in a paper bag with the child's name on it.
7. Take the ornaments home and place them under the Christmas tree until it is time to open presents.

Christmas Symbols
Star:
Appeared over the stable in Bethlehem the night Christ was born. It helped people find Baby Jesus.

Candy Cane:
Is a J for Jesus or a shepherd's crook. White is for the purity of Christ. Large red stripe is for the blood Christ shed. Three thin stripes are for the Trinity.

Tree:

Evergreen is for the everlasting love of Christ. It also reminds us of everlasting life.

Wreath:

Evergreen is for everlasting love of Christ and the roundness is for the circle of love we have around us.

Angel:

One told Mary she would have baby Jesus. They sang the night Jesus was born.

 **HINTS**

1. These make nice gifts for parents.
2. Include a card that explains the meaning of each symbol.
3. You can do this at Easter using Easter symbols.

PRESENTING BIBLE STORIES

Bible stories help children learn to live their lives as God intends. They teach important lessons about Christian values. Through them, children learn about God's everlasting love and learn how to live as courageous and obedient people.

Bible stories can be presented in a variety of ways. Flannel boards, story cards, and props add appeal and variety to the presentation of these stories. See the Appendix for hints and a list of resources for creating flannel board stories.

Many of the stories included here allow for active participation, thus stimulating the learning process that helps children remember them. The use of creative dramatics in storytelling allows children to live these stories. Songs also help stimulate and reinforce children's learning of Bible stories. The songs included here are easy to teach and learn. The lyrics are set to familiar tunes, which eliminates the need to read music or play an instrument.

When sharing Bible stories, avoid having the children take turns reading aloud. This is too much like regular school and leaves many children feeling humiliated when they cannot read as well as others. Read or tell the stories yourself, and allow the children to participate by chanting refrains, doing movements and singing songs.

Each of the stories includes a project. You may also want to use the art projects found in the Bible Art section (pages 53-66). Feel free to adapt projects from one story to another. Or use one of the Bible Puzzles on pages 7-33 that correspond to a specific portion of Scripture.

Patterns may be enlarged or reduced with a copier to fit your needs. Each program is designed to naturally flow from one activity to another. So try to complete the activities in the order listed.

The activities in this section can be used in Sunday school programs, vacation Bible school, youth groups, and Christian day care and school settings.

The following age recommendations are provided: ages 3-6 (preschool, kindergarten), ages 6-8 (grades 1 and 2), ages 8-12 (grades 3-6).

The goal of these lessons is for the children to become familiar with each of the stories presented, to be able to summarize or tell the story in their own words, and to find ways to relate the story to their lives. The projects and activities included with each story help achieve that goal.

SOMETHING EXTRA

The SOMETHING EXTRA activities include a variety of story and song suggestions that can enhance and highlight your Bible lessons.

HINTS

Check your public library for these books and stories. If they do not have the book you need in their collection, ask them to borrow it from another library through interlibrary loan for you. You may wish to add these titles to your church library. For a good way to build your church library, see "The Birthday Book Club" on page 119. Feel free to substitute other stories. Ask your children's librarians for assistance. The book *A to Zoo: Subject Access to Children's Picture Books* is filled with topical lists of books for children. See pages 168-169 for bibliographic information on these books.

THE CREATION

Genesis 1–2:3

Ages 3-12

Make a flannel board version of this story. To make an effective night sky, purchase a large piece of sheer, navy blue, nylon material (enough to cover the flannel board). Glue tiny silver sequins on the fabric to make stars. Attach self-stick navy blue Velcro hook and loop fasteners (rough side) to the top so that it will adhere to your flannel board. Lay the material across the top of the flannel board and gently pull it down into position when it is time to create the night sky with stars. Select patterns from flannel board pattern books (see the Appendix). Use animal print materials and textures available in fabric stores to make animals. Use a glue gun to attach the rough side of a strip of Velcro to each piece of fabric so it will adhere to your flannel board.

When telling the story, ask the children to join you on the refrain, "God was pleased and said, 'This is good!' "

DISCUSSION

Say to young children: "Name things that God has created. What do you like about our world?" Ask older children: "Why did God create the world? Why did God create the things in our world? How can we care for God's creation? How can we make our world a better place to live?"

Explain that God is *still* creating the world. Ask children to share their thoughts.

SOMETHING EXTRA

Songs to Sing:

Sing any of the songs about creation found in the book titled: *Piggyback Songs in Praise of God* compiled by Jean Warren.

Stories to share:

And God Created Squash by Martha Whitmore Hickman.

God created a lovely world. But God was lonesome, so God created people and promised to stay with them all the time.

The Dreamer by Cynthia Rylant

There was an artist who designed a magnificent world. They called the artist God.

Old Turtle by Douglas Wood

One day there was an argument about God. Old Turtle who was usually very quiet, gently answered everyone's questions.

Designed by God, So I Must Be Special by Bonnie Sose

This delightful story about God's magnificent creation helps children understand they are a very special part of God's world.

ART PROJECT: CREATE A MURAL OF CREATION

Ages 3-12

✂ MATERIALS

9 pieces of white construction paper (12" x 18")
Crayons
1-inch squares of green tissue paper for leaves
1-inch squares of colored tissue paper for flowers
Scissors
Glue
Colored markers

📝 PREPARATION

Use markers to print lines from the story across the top and bottom of each page.
On the first page print in the center of the page:

GOD'S CREATION

Second through eighth pages print (across the top of paper):
On the first day, God created
Print across the bottom of paper:
God was pleased and said, 'This is good!' "
Finish the sentence at the top of each page with the following
(Day 1) night and day
(Day 2) sky and water
(Day 3) earth
(Day 4) sun, moon, and stars
(Day 5) birds and fish
(Day 6) animals and people
(Day 7) God rested and enjoyed the world!

1. Give each child a page to illustrate. Encourage the children to draw pictures that depict what is written on their papers. Use tissue paper for flowers and leaves of trees. Show them how to gently squish the tissue paper to make a multidimensional effect. Invite the children to "autograph" their drawings.
2. Along the back tape the mural together in the proper order.
3. Display the mural in a prominent place or send the mural to a friend or church member who is hospitalized or unable to leave home.

Ages 3-12

To make a "Big Book About the Story of Creation," follow the directions for "God's Creation," page 69. Put pages together in order to make a book. Create an attractive cover and back page. Cover both with clear Contact paper. Staple together, or punch holes on the left side and tie with attractive ribbon or fasten with brackets.

✂ VARIATIONS

Ages 6-12

▲ Have the children add their own thoughts (poems, songs, prayers, and so forth) about the things God created.

▲ Create books with drawings of things God has created (for example, trees, mountains, storms, snowflakes, flowers). Write about the selected item.

▲ Choose one aspect of creation (for example, animals, trees, flowers, mountains, children) and draw and write about it.

▲ Create posters that encourage others to love and care for God's creations.

🧩 HINTS

▲ The children may need to do research to complete some of these projects.

▲ To extend this lesson for seven sessions, each child can create his or her own mural or big book. Make one selection/page during each session. Store the pages in the classroom until the book is complete.

▲ Large classes can create several murals or big books as a class. Send the extras to classmates or friends who are at home ill.

▲ Encourage children to use a variety of art materials (for example, crayons, chalk, paints, tissue paper, material scraps) when creating their art projects.

Bible Puzzles
See pages 8-9 for puzzles that accompany this story.

ADAM AND EVE

Genesis 2:4–3:24

Ages 3-12

Tell the story of Adam and Eve. Use the same flannel board pieces from "The Creation." Make figures of Adam and Eve to add to the scene. Also add garden figures.

 **DISCUSSION**

Ask: "Why did God create people? Why does God need us? How can people help God?"

Explain that we are created in God's image. God's image is good. We are born inherently good, but sometimes we choose to disobey, just as Adam and Eve did. When God created us, God gave us the gift of free choice. God can tell us the right things to do, but we still have a choice to make. Will we obey God, or will we disobey?

Talk about how easy it is to disobey even when we know better. Why do we sometimes choose to disobey? What happens when we disobey?

SOMETHING EXTRA

Story to share:
The Naming by Margaret Greaves
Adam named all of the creatures on earth and explained their purpose.

Discussion:
What is our purpose? Each of us has something special to offer. Talk about the different people in your congregation or school, such as the pastor, music director, teachers. What is their purpose? Explain that each of them is special and created in God's image.

Each of us has a purpose, and part of our job is to discover that purpose.

Songs to Sing:
Sing any of these songs from: *Piggyback Songs in Praise of God* compiled by Jean Warren.
"God's Creatures," "Birds and Butterflies," "Gifts of God."

ART PROJECT: CREATION COLLAGES

Ages 3-12

Learning Goal: Children will discover that they are a part of God's creation.

✂ MATERIALS

1 piece of large construction paper per person (12" x 18")
Glue
Magazine pictures of things God has created
Felt markers
Instant camera with film (optional)

PREPARATION

1. Cut pictures from magazines
2. Make individual packets for each child of 15-20 pictures

➡ DIRECTIONS

Give each child a colored sheet of paper, glue, and a packet of pictures. Write the words "GOD CREATED" on the paper. (Do this ahead of time for younger children.) Create a collage using the pictures. Older children may wish to add words to their collages.

✕ VARIATIONS

▲ Make posters to hang in the classroom or hallway
▲ Make "Creation Boxes." Use pictures or artwork to cover a box for storing treasures. Find things God has created to store in your box.
▲ Create a gigantic collage on the wall by using a huge piece of paper and filling it with words and pictures.
▲ Take instant photos of the children while they are working and insert them into their collages.
▲ Take instant photos of the children and make a photo collage.
▲ Make a collage using the color photographs from magazines, photos of the children, children's drawings, and other art materials.

NOAH'S ARK

Genesis 6–9

Ages 3-12

Make a flannel board version of this story, using animal print materials and textures (for example, gray leather for elephants, hippos and rhinos; fur for lions and bears; animal prints for giraffes, tigers). You can also use Pellon nonwoven textile to make animals. See instructions for using Pellon for flannel boards in the Appendix, page 166-67.

There are also Noah's Ark play sets available for purchase in Christian stores and from Christian mail order catalogs. Or use plastic or wooden animals found in toy stores. Children enjoy using these to recreate the story.

Tell the story to the children. Allow them to participate by naming each of the animals as they enter the ark. Children can also make the animal sounds. Each child can make a different sound. Together they can make quite a racket. Add a refrain such as "Imagine all that noise!"

 ## A SONG TO SING

"Animals on the Ark" by Cindy Dingwall
(Sung to "Wheels On the Bus")
The lions on the ark said "Roar, Roar, Roar,"
"Roar, Roar, Roar; Roar, Roar, Roar."
The lions on the ark said, "Roar, Roar, Roar,"
All through the storm.
(Create verses for each animal. This works well on the flannel board. Add each animal as you sing about it. Have children move like the animals.)

 ## HINT

Sing this song as you tell the story.

 ## DISCUSSION

Ask: "Why was God angry at the people on earth? Why did God choose Noah and his family to take the animals on the ark? Why did God tell Noah to take two of each animal?" If any of the children have experienced a flood, ask them to share what it was like. What happened? How did they feel? What was the outcome?

SOMETHING EXTRA

Stories to share:
Why Noah Chose the Dove by Isaac Bashevis Singer
When the animals learned that Noah was building the ark, they began to argue about who should be taken along. Only the dove remained quiet. It was she whom Noah chose to be the messenger.
Noah & the Ark & the Animals by Andrew Elborn
During a frightening storm, a mother horse comforts her colt by telling him a story about another storm that happened many years ago.
Noah's Ark by Peter Spier
Lovely illustrations tell this story about how Noah and his family escaped the storm. (This is also available as a book/cassette package. The cassette includes marvelous sound effects.)
Noah's Ark Illuminated by Isabelle Brent
Striking illustrations add a new dimension to the story of Noah and the flood.
Rise and Shine by Fiona French
This humorous retelling of Noah's Ark can be used in connection with the song below.
Song to Sing:
"Arky, Arky"
(from the book: ***Sing 'n' Celebrate for Kids,*** Volume 2)

DRAMATIC PLAY: ACT OUT THE STORY OF "NOAH'S ARK"

Ages 3-12

Have the children create masks to dramatize this story. Older children can play the parts of Noah and his family.

MAKING ANIMAL MASKS

Ages 3-12

✂ MATERIALS

1 paper plate per animal (child)
Construction paper in a variety of colors
Crayons
Scissors
Glue
Stapler and staples
Yarn
Hole punch

▶ DIRECTIONS

Decide which animals to use and who will portray them. You will need two of each animal. Hold a paper plate up to child's face, and use a pencil to mark where the eyes will go. Help child cut out the eye holes. Use construction paper to make ears, noses, mouths, trunks, manes, and so forth. Have the children use crayons to color their masks. Glue or staple ears, noses, mouths, trunks, manes to the mask. Punch one hole on each side of the mask. Attach yarn. Put the mask on the child and tie it in the back of the head.

⊰ HINTS

Let children create their masks without the use of patterns. This aids their creativity and makes for very interesting and unique animals.

Books of ready-made animal masks can be purchased in bookstores. You can also purchase costume masks at post-Halloween sales.

Act out the story, using blocks to build the ark. Make the song "Animals on the Ark" (page 73) part of the drama.

The narrator says:

"God was very unhappy with the way people on earth were behaving. God decided to destroy all living things on earth. God was pleased with Noah who was obedient. God decided to let Noah and his family survive the flood, so God instructed Noah to build an ark."

(Noah and his family build an ark out of the blocks.)

Continue telling the story using your own words and encouraging children to act out their parts.

💡 IDEA

This makes a great presentation for a school assembly, a parent's night program, or a Sunday school program given for the congregation during worship.

ART PROJECT: NOAH'S ARK MOBILE

Ages 3-12

✂ MATERIALS

One precut white dove per child
One precut uncolored rainbow per child
One precut uncolored ark per child
Precut animal shapes (10 per child/2 shapes of 5 different animals)
(Ideas: giraffe; tiger; elephant; bear; hippo; birds—raven, sea gull; lion; donkey)
(See Appendix "Resources for Creating Flannel Board Stories," *Mix and Match Series,* on page 167.)
Crayons
13 six-inch pieces of thick yarn per child
Hole punch

PREPARATION

1. Punch a hole in the top and bottom of the dove and rainbow.
2. Punch one hole in the top of the ark and ten across the bottom.
3. Punch holes in the tops of the animals.

➡ DIRECTIONS

Have the children color the ark and rainbow. Ask the children to neatly print their name on the ark. (Assist younger children.) Give each child a packet of ten animals to color. String the mobiles (The dove goes on top with the rainbow underneath. Under the rainbow is the ark. The ten animals are attached to the ark. Vary the lengths of yarn when adding the animals. Yes, it will be crowded, but that's how it was on the ark . . . crowded.

✄ VARIATIONS:

Ages 3-12

▲ Make a Noah's Ark Mural following the instructions for creating murals found in "Bible Art" on page 57.
▲ Use the Noah's Ark theme to register Sunday school, class, or kid's club attendance. Create an ocean scene using blue paper cut to resemble waves. Make a stormy sky scene with clouds and rain. Put an ark on the water with a plank leading up to it. When children arrive, they can choose an animal (provide two of each animal), write their name on it and add it to the procession going onto the ark. Children can do this each week for a quarter, semester, or the entire year. See how long the line of animals
is . . . and how many different species of animals you can represent.

Ages 6-12

▲ Ask the children to do animal reports. Choose an animal and research it. Draw pictures of the animal, and tell why *you* think this animal was chosen to go on the ark.
▲ Draw a picture of your animal and write a poem about it.

💡 IDEA

See the Bible Puzzles on pages 9-10 that can be used with this story.

JACOB'S LADDER

Genesis 28:10-22

Ages 3-12

Place a real ladder that goes from the floor to the ceiling in your classroom. Make clouds out of batting material available in fabric stores. Suspend them from the ceiling so they cover the top rung of the ladder. Purchase a variety of large angels (look for post-Christmas sales). Set the angels on the rungs of the ladder to illustrate the story. Tell the story to the children using the ladder and angels as props.

DISCUSSION

Talk about how God is with us everywhere we go. God is always there to help us. Ask "Can you think of times when God has helped you? Think of a time when you were really scared or sad. How did God help you?" Explain that God sends other people to help us. When we are hurt or sick, parents and other adults care for us. With older children, discuss how angels help people. With the aid of a concordance show children other instances in the Bible when angels helped people.

SOMETHING EXTRA

▲ Visit the bookstore or library for books about angel encounters. Choose stories of how angels are said to have helped people. Share them with the children. Ask if *they* feel they have been helped by an angel.

▲ Talk about guardian angels. "How do they help us?"

▲ Let the children create and illustrate stories about how angels could help people.

▲ Have children find an angel book to read and discuss.

A SONG TO SING

"We Are Climbing Jacob's Ladder" by Cindy Dingwall
  (Sung to "Mary Had a Little Lamb")
We are climbing Jacob's ladder, Jacob's ladder, Jacob's ladder.
  We are climbing Jacob's ladder.
  How high can we go?
We are climbing higher, higher, higher, higher, higher, higher.
  We are climbing higher, higher.
  How high can we go?
    God goes with me everywhere, everywhere, everywhere.
  God goes with me everywhere.
  God takes good care of me!

ART PROJECT: ANGELS ON THE LADDER

Ages 3-6

MATERIALS

A picture of a ladder (one per child)
Angel stickers or pictures (5-10 per child)
Glue

DIRECTIONS

Give each child a picture of a ladder and some angel stickers or pictures. Help them glue or stick the angels on the ladder.

ART PROJECT: JACOB'S LADDER

Ages 6-12

MATERIALS

Craft sticks
Glue
Small angels (can be stickers, pictures cut from cards, and so forth)

DIRECTIONS

Give each child a batch of craft sticks. Show children how to construct a ladder from their craft sticks. Have them glue the ladder together and glue angels to the ladder. Dry flat for 24 hours.

IDEA

See pages 11-12 for puzzles that accompany this story.

JOSEPH AND THE COAT OF MANY COLORS

Genesis 37–43

Ages 3-12

Make story cards for this story. Find a Bible story coloring book that features this story. Purchase two copies. Color each picture and use rubber cement to mount on colored construction paper. Leave a border of each picture. Write the text across the back of each picture. Or, find an inexpensive paperback edition of this story, purchase two copies, cut out each picture, and mount them on construction paper. Number the pictures on the back, so the story stays in proper order.

DISCUSSION

Discuss how Joseph's brothers treated him. Is that how God wants us to treat our brothers and sisters? Talk about how Joseph acted. Did Joseph's actions please God?

HINT

There are many elements in this story. Pick one or two to focus on and design your discussion around those points.

SOMETHING EXTRA

Songs to Sing:
Sing any of the songs about Joseph and his colorful coat found in the book, *Piggyback Songs in Praise of God* compiled by Jean Warren.

ART PROJECT: _____'S COAT OF MANY COLORS

Ages 3-12

MATERIALS

1 discarded white long-sleeve shirt per child (older children may prefer to use T-shirts)
Fabric paints, fabric crayons and glitter in as many colors as possible
Glue
Black markers
1 hanger per child

DIRECTIONS

Use marker to print child's name on the collar of the shirt.
Let the children design their own multicolored coat. Put each child's coat on a hanger to dry.

VARIATIONS

Ages 3-8

During Parent's Night or the worship service have the children wear their coats and sing one of the songs they learned.

Ages 8-12

If there is a production of the musical *Joseph and the Amazing Technicolor Dreamcoat* playing nearby, arrange a group outing to see it. Listen to the recording of it beforehand.

IDEA

See page 12-13 for puzzles that accompany this story. To make this project in multiple sessions, do one side the first session, and the other side during the second session.

THE TEN COMMANDMENTS

Exodus 20:1-17

Ages 3-12

This story is probably one of the most important lessons in the Bible. Plan to spend several weeks learning about the Ten Commandments and the valuable lessons they teach us. Focus on one or two commandments per session.

Make two large tablets out of plaster of Paris by mixing according to the directions and pouring into disposable aluminum foil pans (9" x 13"). Let them set. Remove them from the pans. Paint them light gray if desired. Once dry, use a permanent black marker to write the Ten Commandments on them.

Show and read the tablets to the children. Let the children feel how heavy these tablets are. Let them see how the commandments are written on them. Read or tell the story to the children.

DISCUSSION

Ask: "Why did God give us the Ten Commandments? Why do we need to have rules? How do rules help us? How do rules keep us safe from harm?"

Talk about what happens when we don't follow rules. Ask: "What are some of the consequences? How do you feel when you have broken a rule?"

SOMETHING EXTRA

Stories to share:

A Book About God by Florence Mary Fitch

God is special. We can see God in everything.

Discuss how this book applies to the first commandment.

King Midas and the Golden Touch by Kathryn Hewitt

King Midas worshiped gold more than anything else. When he accidentally turned his beloved daughter into a gold statue, he realized how wrong he had been.

Discuss why we should worship God rather than things. Focus on the second commandment.

Elbert's Bad Word by Audrey Wood

Elbert had horrified everyone by saying a bad word.

Discuss why God wants us to avoid using bad language. Apply this to the third commandment.

Forest of Dreams by Rosemary Wells

A young girl is thankful for all of the beautiful things in her life.

Discuss why it is important to spend time with God. "Why do we need to go to church and worship God?" Use this to discuss the fourth commandment.

I'll Fix Anthony by Judith Viorst

A young boy thinks about how he will get even with his brother.

Talk about the normal feelings of anger we have toward one another at times. "How can we deal with these feelings in a way that will not harm someone?" Apply this to the sixth commandment.

Arnie and the Stolen Markers by Nancy Carlson

Arnie stole a set of markers from the store. He felt so guilty that he finally had to confess. He was punished but learned a valuable lesson.

Discuss what happens when we steal. Cheating in school is also a form of stealing. "What can we do so we remember not to steal?" Focus on the eighth commandment.

A Big, Fat Enormous Lie by Marjorie Sharmat

A child had told a lie. The lie grew so big and bothersome that the child could only do one thing . . . tell the truth.

Discuss what happens when we lie. "How do we feel? How do others respond when we lie? How do they feel about us when they discover we have lied? Can we trust people who lie? Why not?" Focus on the ninth commandment.

Frog in the Middle by Susanna Gretz

The three friends learn to deal with all sorts of problems including jealousy.

Talk about how it feels to be jealous. What can we do when we feel jealous? How can we help someone who feels jealous? Look at the tenth commandment.

 ## A SONG TO SING

"The Ten Commandments" by Cindy Dingwall
   (Sung to "Mary Had a Little Lamb")
   God gave Moses Ten Commandments, Ten Commandments, Ten Commandments.
   God gave Moses Ten Commandments; this is what God said.
   We must worship only God, only God, only God.
   We must worship only God;
   That is commandment one.

   God said not to worship things, worship things, worship things.
   God said not to worship things;
   That is commandment two.

   God said not to use bad words, use bad words, use bad words.
   God says not to use bad words;
   That is commandment three.

   God said we must go to church, go to church, go to church.
   God said we must go to church;
   That is commandment four.

God said we must honor parents, honor parents, honor parents.
God said we must honor parents;
That is commandment five.

God said we are not to kill, not to kill, not to kill.
God said we are not to kill;
That is commandment six.

God said we must honor marriage, honor marriage, honor marriage.
God said we must honor marriage;
That is commandment seven.

God said we are not to steal, not to steal, not to steal.
God said we are not to steal;
That is commandment eight.

God said we are not to lie, not to lie, not to lie.
God said we are not to lie;
That is commandment nine.

God said we should not be jealous, not be jealous, not be jealous.
God said we should not be jealous;
That is commandment ten.

Ten Commandments help us live, help us live, help us live.
Ten Commandments help us live,
Just the way God wants.

TEN COMMANDMENTS SCROLL

Ages 3-12

MATERIALS

2 cardboard paper towel tubes per person
13 pieces of beige parchment paper per person
   (can be found in office/art supply stores)
Brown crayons (several different shades of brown)
Tape (regular and book tape)
Brown felt markers
1 24" strand of brown yarn per person
Pencils

➡ DIRECTIONS

1. Give each person a blank piece of paper and have each write "THE TEN COMMANDMENTS" across the middle using a brown felt marker. Decorate with brown crayons.
2. On the second piece of paper, have students use a pencil to write the first commandment. Trace over the pencil lines with brown marker. Decorate with brown crayons.
3. Follow the same procedure with the second through tenth commandments. For younger children write the commandments and allow the children to decorate each page.
4. When all pages are complete, use regular tape to tape them together in the proper order. Tape along the edges of the paper, joining them into a scroll. Add the title page, and one extra blank page to the beginning and end of the scroll. Use book tape to attach the scroll to the cardboard tubes. String the length of brown yarn through the top tube and tie. The scrolls can be rolled up and carried home and used as a wall hanging.

✂ HINT

Since this project will take several sessions, keep the papers at school until the project is completed.

✕ VARIATIONS

Ages 8-12

▲ Make tablets rather than scrolls. See directions for making tablets on page 79.
Create books by having students
▲ Write essays on the importance of obeying the Ten Commandments. Assign a different commandment to each child. Compile these into a book to add to the church library.
▲ Write poetry about the commandments. Illustrate your work. Compile this into a book, and add it to the church library.
▲ Write stories about the fifth and seventh commandments. Share these with the younger children.

💡 IDEA

See page 14-15 for puzzles that accompany this story.

JONAH AND THE WHALE

Book of Jonah
Ages 3-12

Create a large whale from black poster board with a see-through stomach and a large mouth. Make a stick puppet of Jonah using a craft stick and drawing.

✂ MATERIALS

2 extra-large pieces of black, heavy-duty poster board
1 large Ziploc storage bag
1 large piece of white paper the same size as the poster board
1 piece of white construction paper
Crayons
Scissors
Glue
Book tape
Craft sticks
Clear Contact paper
Waxed paper
Patterns of whale and Jonah (Appendix pages 172-73)
   (Enlarge on copier)

▶ DIRECTIONS

Use the whale pattern to draw a large whale on the large piece of white paper. (See pattern on page 173. Be sure to leave the mouth open.) Cut it out.
Lay the pattern on top of black poster board and trace it. Cut out two identical whales. Draw an opening in the stomach and cut it out from both pieces. Cut the Ziploc bag apart, and tape it over the stomach opening that will be inside the whale. Cover both pieces of the whale, making sure to tape down all edges. Make eyes and teeth from white construction paper. Glue the teeth to the inside of the mouth. Tape down the edges. Glue the eyes to both sides of the outside of the whale. Cut 6 strips 6" x ½" of waxed paper. Band together with tape. Tape to one side of the inside of the whale, so it looks as though the whale is spouting. Glue the whale together (a glue gun works well for this).
Copy the pattern of Jonah. Color, cut, and cover it with clear Contact paper. Use book tape to secure it to a craft stick.
Jonah will slip in and out of the whale's mouth. The plastic will enable children to see Jonah inside the whale's stomach. (Allow whale to dry at least 24 hours before using.) Tell the story using your newly created whale as a prop.

🙌 DISCUSSION

Ask the children to share their impressions of this story. "Do you think it really happened? Why or why not? Why do you think God wants us to know this story? What does it teach us about God? Do you think God always forgives us?"

🎁 SOMETHING EXTRA

Stories to Share:
The Book of Jonah by Peter Spier
   Peter Spier's paintings add a fascinating dimension to this timeless tale.
Jonah and the Great Fish by Warwick Hutton
   Lovely illustrations highlight this wonderful story.
The Story of Jonah by Kurt Baumann
   Beautiful illustrations bring this tale of adventure to life for young readers.

A Song to Sing:
"Jonah" found in the book ***Piggyback Songs in Praise of God*** compiled by Jean Warren.

ART PROJECT: JONAH AND THE WHALE

Ages 3-12

The children can create their own whales using the instructions on page 82. Theirs can be about half the size of yours. Provide precut whales with the plastic stomach attached. Give each child a piece of white paper with patterns for the eyes, teeth, and Jonah.

Give each child a copy of the story to take home with the whale.

 IDEA

See pages 15-16 for puzzles that accompany this story.

THE BIRTH OF JESUS

Matthew 1:18–2:12; Luke 2:1-20

Ages 3-12

These lessons are designed to be used during the four-week Advent season. Explain that advent means waiting. Tell or read the story of Christmas.

 **DISCUSSION**

Ask: "Have any of you ever welcomed a new baby into your family? How did it feel to wait for the new baby to arrive? What was it like when the baby arrived? How do you think Mary and Joseph felt while they were waiting? What do you think they thought when God told them Jesus would be very special?"

Explain why Jesus is special to us.

SOMETHING EXTRA

Story to Share:
Christmas by Jan Pienkowski
Striking illustrations silhouetted against painted background provides a breathtaking look at this story.

Other stories to share:
Mary of Nazareth by Cecil Bodker (ages 8-12)
The Nativity story told from Mary's perspective provides added insight to the birth of Jesus.
How the Hibernators Came to Bethlehem by Norma Farber
A beautiful star shone in the sky awakening the animals from their winter nap. Guided by the star, they journeyed to a stable in Bethlehem where they found a tiny baby.
All Those Mothers at the Manger by Norma Farber (ages 3-6)
The stable was filled with other mothers on that night. They all shared in the joy of Jesus' birth.
The Christmas Star by Marcus Pfister
The star was magnificent, unlike anything they had ever seen. Join the followers of the star.

Songs to Sing:
Sing any of the Christmas songs found in the book: *Piggyback Songs in Praise of Jesus.* These songs make a nice addition to a Christmas pageant.

ART PROJECT: CHRISTMAS STORY MURAL

Ages 3-12

 MATERIALS

5 precut frames per child (use cover stock paper)
Precut patterns of the following: Joseph and Mary looking at Jesus lying in the manger, star, shepherd, Three Wise Men, donkey. Each person will need a packet containing all five. See Appendix pages 174-77.
Crayons
Glue
Glitter
Book tape

DIRECTIONS

Give each child a packet of patterns to color. Put glitter on the star. Give everyone five frames. Have the children glue one picture inside each frame.
Tape the frames together so the story is in the proper sequence. (Use book tape, taping along the back of the frames.)

Christmas Story Mural
Allow the children to tell the story in their own words. Stand the murals on a table as a Christmas decoration or give them to parents as gifts.

VARIATIONS

Ages 8-12

▲ Ask the children to imagine themselves as Mary or Joseph. Answer these questions, "How would it feel to be visited by an angel and told you were going to have the baby Jesus? How would you feel if you were going to be father of this child?"
▲ Write essays on their thoughts and feelings about the Christmas story.
▲ Create their own illustrations rather than using patterns for the story murals.

HINT

After-Christmas sales provide an excellent source for pictures you need for this project. Purchase boxes of cards that can be used or ask people to donate old Christmas cards.

CHRISTMAS CAROLS

Ages 6-12

DIRECTIONS

Help children learn about the history and origins of favorite Christmas carols. They can also learn to sing each carol.

 SOMETHING EXTRA

These books include many fascinating facts about carols.
Tasha Tudor's Favorite Christmas Carols by Tasha Tudor
A Treasury of Christmas Songs and Carols by Harry W. Simon

ART PROJECT: SONG PICTURES

Ages 6-12

**MATERIALS**

1 large piece of white construction paper per person
Crayons
Pencils

DIRECTIONS

Ask the children to draw an illustration of their favorite Christmas carol. Have them write the name of the carol and tell why they like it. (Younger children may need assistance.) Sing some of the carols.

CHRISTMAS SYMBOLS

Ages 3-12

Talk about the meanings of Christmas symbols: *wreath, tree, star of Bethlehem, candy cane, poinsettia, bells, candle, holly, angels, and so forth.*

**SOMETHING EXTRA**

Holly, Reindeer, and Colored Lights by Edna Barth
   Use this book to explain the meaning and history of Christmas symbols.

ART PROJECT: CHRISTMAS RIBBONS

Ages 3-12

✂ MATERIALS

Several spools of Christmas ribbon [craft/fabric stores] (Each child will need a piece of ribbon 1-inch wide by 3-feet long.)
8 precut paper circles per child—4" in diameter. See Appendix page 175. Printed explanations of each Christmas symbol—1 sheet per child (see Bible Art page 65-66)
Pictures of Christmas symbols—4 per child (see Patterns, Appendix page 197)
Crayons
Glue
Scissors
Clear Contact paper or laminating film (optional)

PREPARATION

1. Cut ribbon into three foot lengths.
2. Tie a loop at the top for hanging.
3. Prepare for each child a packet containing four of the five symbols and their explanations.

➡ DIRECTIONS

Have the children
1. Color the four symbols.
2. Cut them out and glue them to the circles.
3. Glue (or staple) the circles with the pictures to the ribbon. Allow 2" between circles.
4. Glue the explanations to the remaining circles.
5. Glue (or staple) the circles with the explanations to the back of the ribbon, taking care to match the explanation with its picture.

HINTS

1. Help children with cutting as needed.
2. To make these last, laminate circles (or cover with clear Contact paper) before attaching them to the ribbons. These make great gifts.

ART PROJECT: MAKING CHRISTMAS CARDS

Ages 3-12

 MATERIALS

Construction paper in assorted colors (one sheet per child—they may choose their own color)
Crayons and markers
Pencils
Glue
Glitter

▶ DIRECTIONS

Have the children fold the paper, draw pictures, and write a message to create a Christmas card. Have children sign their cards.

Send the cards to

▲ Classmates who are sick or hospitalized.
▲ Members of the congregation who are ill.
▲ Children in a local hospital or homeless shelter.
▲ Residents of a nursing home, retirement facility, or veteran's hospital who are without family.
▲ People serving in the armed forces.

💡 IDEA

See pages 17-18 for puzzles that accompany this story.

THE BEATITUDES

Matthew 5:3-12

Ages 8-12

This lesson can cover a period of several weeks. Plan to cover two Beatitudes per week.

Read the scripture. Explain that we cannot receive God's blessings unless we need them, and all of us need God's blessings. Talk about the Beatitudes. Ask, "What does each one mean? Can we think of ways to put them into our own words?"

Talk about times when you have experienced similar feelings to those discussed in the Beatitudes. Explain how God helped you. Ask the children to share similar experiences. This is one of the most comforting passages in the New Testament. Jesus gave the Sermon on the Mount to reassure us of God's everlasting love for us.

 A SONG TO SING

"Rejoice and Be Glad" by Cindy Dingwall
   (Sung to "Michael, Row the Boat")
   Rejoice and be glad, Alleluia
   Rejoice and be glad, Alleluia

God helps the poor in spirit, Alleluia
God helps the poor in spirit, Alleluia
God comforts they who mourn, Alleluia
God comforts they who mourn, Alleluia
God asks us to be meek, Alleluia
God asks us to be meek, Alleluia
God nourishes our soul, Alleluia
God nourishes our soul, Alleluia
God is so merciful, Alleluia
God is so merciful, Alleluia
God wants us to be pure, Alleluia
God wants us to be pure, Alleluia
God wants us to make peace, Alleluia
God wants us to make peace, Alleluia
God helps us when we suffer, Alleluia
God helps us when we suffer, Alleluia
Rejoice and be glad, Alleluia
Rejoice and be glad, Alleluia

ART PROJECT: BEATITUDES WALL HANGING

Ages 8-12

✂ MATERIALS

1 piece of gray poster board cut into the shape of a mountain.
Write the words: *The Sermon on the Mount.* Across the top middle
portion of the mountain, print *The Beatitudes* directly underneath.
1 piece of white poster board cut into the shape of a cloud. Write:
Rejoice and Be Glad! on the front of the cloud.
8 pieces of white cover stock paper (8" x 2")
2 pieces of ribbon—2" x 36" [may be purchased at a fabric or craft
store]
Crayons
Book tape
Staples
Glue
Pencils
Crayola Markers—bold colors
Small nails and hammer
2 six-inch strands of yarn looped and tied to make a hanger

PREPARATION

Use pencil to lightly draw two lines across each rectangle.

➡ DIRECTIONS

1. Give each child a rectangle, a pencil, and a Beatitude to copy
   from the Bible.
2. Ask the children to copy the Beatitude onto the rectangle. Trace
   over the pencil lines with colored marker. Use crayons to
   decorate your Beatitude.
3. Attach the two pieces of long ribbon to the mountain with book
   tape, staples, or glue.

4. Attach the Beatitudes to the two pieces of ribbon in the proper
   order, leaving about 1 inch between each.
5. Attach the cloud to the bottom of the ribbons.
6. Allow 24 hours to dry. Attach the yarn
   hanger to the back of the mountain
   with book tape. Hammer a
   small nail into the wall,
   and hang.

💡 IDEA

See page 18 for a
puzzle that
accompanies this
story.

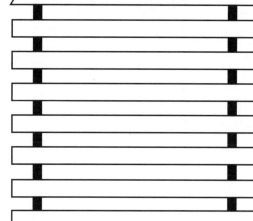

Sermon
on the Mount
The Beatitudes

Rejoice and Be Glad!

THE GOLDEN RULE

Matthew 7:12

Ages 6-12

Read this passage of scripture. Explain that God wants us to treat each other with kindness and respect and to be willing to help one another.

DISCUSSION

Ask children to share instances when they have seen people practice and *not* practice the Golden Rule. Ask: "How do you feel about what you saw? What would you do differently?"

SOMETHING EXTRA

Songs to Sing:
"Be Kind," "Show Love to Everyone," "Jesus Said," "Let's Be Kind," and "Let's Be Good" all found in the book *Piggyback Songs in Praise of Jesus* compiled by Jean Warren

Story to Share:
Do You Know What I'll Do? by Charlotte Zolotow
A little girl tells her brother about all of the things she will do for him.
Talk about ways you can *live* "The Golden Rule."

ART PROJECT: GOLDEN RULE MOBILE

Ages 6-12

 MATERIALS

1 large white cloud per person (cut from white poster board)
2 small white clouds per person (cut from white poster board)
Yarn
Glue
Gold glitter
1 gold glitter crayon per person
Blow dryer
Hole punch

PREPARATION

1. Punch a hole in the top center of the large cloud. Punch two holes along the bottom of the large cloud. Punch holes in the top center of both small clouds.
2. Use a pencil to lightly print the words: "THE GOLDEN RULE" on both sides of the large white cloud. Print the words "Do unto others" on both sides of one of the smaller clouds. Print the words "As you would have them do unto you" on both sides of the other small cloud.

➡ DIRECTIONS

1. Give each person a large cloud, a small bottle of glue, and a container of gold glitter. Have the children place glue on the letters, sprinkle with gold glitter, and set aside to dry. Have them use gold crayon to go over the words on the two smaller clouds.
2. Read a story or sing a song while the glue dries. Have children glue and glitter the words on the second side of the large cloud. Help them string yarn through the top hole of the large cloud and attach the two smaller clouds to the top cloud with yarn.

💡 IDEA

See page 19 for a puzzle that accompanies this story.

HINT

Use a blow dryer to dry the glue.

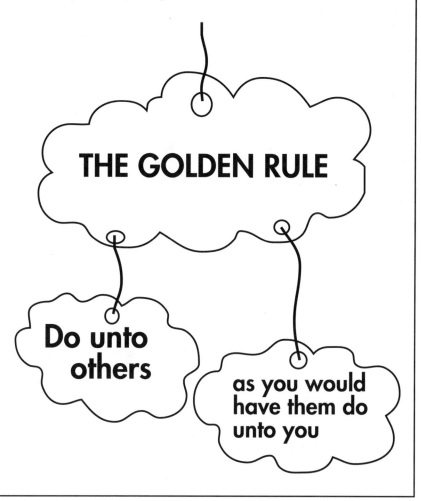

THE LORD'S PRAYER

Matthew 6:9-13

Ages 6-12

Read the scripture to the children. Jesus taught us to pray this prayer to God. Explain the meaning of this prayer. We are talking to God in heaven. We are asking God to help us do the Lord's will. We ask God to provide the food we need to eat. We ask to be forgiven for our sins and promise to forgive others. We ask God to help keep us from being tempted to do wrong things, and to keep us free from sin. We recognize that God is in charge of our world. The word *AMEN* means "so be it."

DISCUSSION

Ask the children to share their thoughts about this prayer. Remind them of the Creation story where God created plants and animals. "Does God provide the food we need? Who creates plants and animals today?"

Talk about forgiveness. "Do your parents forgive you when you have done something wrong? Do others forgive you? Do you forgive others? How does it feel to be forgiven? Why? How does it feel when someone does not forgive you? Why? What does God tell us about forgiveness?"

Talk about temptation. "Have you ever been tempted to do something wrong? What was it? What happened? How did you feel? What can we do when we are tempted to do something wrong?"

Be willing to share your thoughts and experiences. Children need to know that adults face the same kinds of things that they do.

SOMETHING EXTRA

Songs to Sing:

"The Lord's Prayer" by Malotte. Ask your choir director to have the adult choir lead the congregation in singing "The Lord's Prayer." The congregation has heard it enough that, led by the choir, they will be able to sing it. The children will learn to sing it after hearing it sung a few times. Children are fascinated when they hear this prayer sung rather than spoken.

"Talked to Jesus" found in the book *Piggyback Songs in Praise of Jesus* compiled by Jean Warren.

"I Praise God Every Day" found in the book *Piggyback Songs in Praise of God* compiled by Jean Warren.

ACTIVITY: A STORY ABOUT PRAYER

Ages 6-12

Have the children create a story about prayer. These can be personal experience stories or make-believe, but *must* be Christian in context.

For example: Help students compose a story about another child who prays to God. What does the child pray for? How does God answer that prayer? What happens?

Ask the children to illustrate the stories. Make an attractive cover, and add a plain back sheet. Staple the sheets together, and each child will have a book about prayer.

 ## HINT

Let children who are just learning to read and write (or those who have difficulty) dictate their stories.

ART PROJECT: LORD'S PRAYER PLAQUE

Ages 6-12

 ## MATERIALS

Typed copy of the Lord's Prayer (one per person)
1 piece of plywood per person—8" x 10"

Wood grain spray paint	Colored pencils
Decoupage solution	Paint brushes with fat bristles
Picture hangers	Markers

PREPARATION

1. Spray paint each of the plaques with wood grain spray paint. (Do this outdoors.) Let them dry 24 hours.
2. Attach picture hangers to the back of the plaque.
3. Prepare copies of the Lord's Prayer. Choose an attractive, but easily readable font. Leave a one-inch border around the edges of the paper.

DIRECTIONS

Give each child a copy of the prayer and colored pencils. Have them draw a decorative border around the prayer. Have the children use a marker to write their name on the back of the plaque.

Laminate each prayer (or cover with clear Contact paper)

Center and attach the prayer to the plaques using the decoupage solution. Lay plaques flat to dry for 24 hours. These make lovely gifts for parents.

IDEA

See page 19 for a puzzle that accompanies this story.

LENTEN ACTIVITIES

During Lent the lessons focus on the miracles of Jesus. On Palm Sunday there is a special project that reflects the miracles of Christ.

Impress upon the children that miracles still occur today. Springtime is filled with the miracle of new growth. Rainbows are miracles. Snowflakes, each one different and unique, are miracles. New babies are miracles. Ask the children to think of other miracles.

WEEK 1: FEEDING OF THE FIVE THOUSAND

Matthew 14:15-21, Mark 6:35-44, Luke 9:12-17, John 6:5-14

Ages 3-12

Tell this story to the children.

DISCUSSION

"How do you think Jesus did this? How did two fish and five loaves of bread feed five thousand people? Do you think that could happen today? Why or why not?"

SOMETHING EXTRA

A story to share:

Stone Soup by Marcia Brown

A man arrived in the village. No one was willing to share their food with him, so he told them he was going to make stone soup. He made enough to feed everyone in town!

Tell this story using a big soup pot, plastic vegetables and a stone. Give each child a vegetable to add.

DISCUSSION

"How did the man make enough soup to feed everyone in the town? How did sharing help everyone? Why is it helpful to share with one another?"

Songs to Sing:

Sing any of these songs while covering the Grace Cards with clear Contact paper (see page 96): "Jesus Fed the Five Thousand," "Five Little Loaves" or "Feeding the Five Thousand" found in *Piggyback Songs in Praise of Jesus* compiled by Jean Warren.

ACTIVITY: "FEEDING THE KIDS"

Ages 3-12

Make a batch of brownies. Cut the brownies and give them to only half of the children. Tell them to wait until you tell them to begin eating. There will be comments about not having enough. Ask the children what to do about this situation. When they come up with the answer, cut each brownie in half and see that everyone receives one.

Ask the children what happened. "First there weren't enough brownies, and then there were enough brownies for all of us. Why? Do you think the people in the story about feeding the five thousand shared the food? How does God feel when we share? Who provides the food for us to eat? What does God want us to do if we have food, but notice that someone else does not?"

HINT

Before using this activity, make sure no one is allergic to chocolate. If so, substitute a food that *all* children can enjoy.

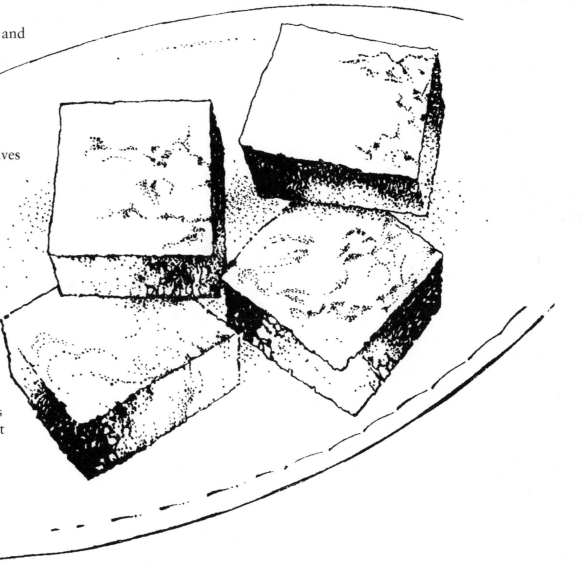

ART PROJECT: GRACE CARDS

Ages 3-12

MATERIALS

1 piece of cover stock paper per child (8" x 10")
Crayons
Glue
Clear Contact paper
White typing paper (6" x 8")
Colored marker

PREPARATION

Precut Contact paper into pieces large enough to cover the Grace Cards. Keep the backing on until it is time to cover the cards.

DIRECTIONS

Compose a group grace. Let each child make suggestions. (Help younger children think of ideas.) Neatly print the grace in the center of the sheet of typing paper. Make copies, and cut the sheets so they are 6" x 8." Give each child one copy, and let them draw a decorative border around it. Glue the prayers to the cover stock paper, leaving an even border around the edges. Write children's names on the back of the card. Cover each grace card with clear Contact paper. Let the children take their cards home to use at mealtime with their families.

VARIATIONS

▲ Let every child compose an individual grace. Make enough copies of each grace so each child can have a copy of all the graces. Have the children decorate each card and glue it to a piece of cover stock paper. Punch two holes across the top of the cards and string with yarn to make a booklet. Make individual covers for the books.

▲ Let each person make a grace card, but have them choose a specific topic: Thanksgiving, Christmas, Easter, Mother's Day, Father's Day, Breakfasts, Lunches, Dinners, Graces for Guests, Picnics, and so forth. Compile these into a book for each child to take home.

These books make nice Easter gifts for parents.

IDEAS

See pages 20-21 for puzzles that accompany this story.
Ask your pastor if the children can share their grace with the congregation.

WEEK 2: JESUS HEALS PEOPLE

Matthew 8:1-4, 14-17; 9:1-8, 18-22, 27-34; and others

Ages 3-12

Talk about all of the people Jesus healed. Choose one of the stories and tell it to the children.

DISCUSSION

Ask the children to share their thoughts and feelings about the story.

Talk about how God and doctors help us get well when we are sick. Ask the children to tell you about times when they have been sick. "What was it like to be sick? How did you feel? Who helped you get better? What did you have to do to get well?" Remind children that we need doctors and parents to help us get well. Sometimes we have to take medicine, stay home, or stay inside.

Ask children if they remember the story of the Creation. "Who created us? Since God created us, we need to let God help us get well. The doctors and our parents will help us too."

Let children share experiences, thoughts and feelings about parents, friends, or relatives who have been ill.

Pray for those on your prayer list who are ill. The children can add other names.

Older children may ask what happens when someone develops a terminal illness or dies explain: "Sometimes we cannot be cured here on earth. God needs to take us to heaven. When we go to heaven to live with God, we know that we will never be sick again. We don't know why some people can be cured here and others cannot. There are just some answers we do not have." Reassure children that most of the time we do recover from our illnesses.

SOMETHING EXTRA

Songs to sing:
"The Blind Men" and "Raising of Jairus' Daughter" from *Piggyback Songs in Praise of Jesus* compiled by Jean Warren.

ART PROJECT: GET-WELL CARDS

Ages 3-12

✂ MATERIALS

Construction paper—8" x 8" (when folded in half it fits into
   4⅛" x 9½" envelope)
Crayons
Markers
List of people in your congregation who are ill
Stickers (optional)
Glitter
Colored tissue paper
Glue
Scissors
Pencils
Envelopes—4⅛" x 9½"
Stamps

PREPARATION

1. Fold construction paper in half.
2. Address and stamp envelopes.

➡ DIRECTIONS

Have the children create get-well cards for those who are ill. For
people who are terminally ill, make a thinking-of-you card. They
can use crayons, stickers (optional), tissue paper, and glitter to
design the cards.

Sign the cards: "From the children in (class or group name)." Ask
each child to sign his or her name to the lower portion of the back
of the card (as the card's designer). Mail the cards.

💡 IDEA

See pages 21-23 for puzzles that accompany this story.

Matthew 14:22-36
Ages 3-12

Borrow a rowboat. Set it in the middle of your classroom, surrounded with bunched-up pieces of blue tissue paper. Over the blue tissue paper stretch blue plastic food wrap. Tape it to the walls and to the sides of the boat. Leave one opening (the shore) so children can enter the boat. Ask a young adult man to dress as Jesus.

Have the children get inside the rowboat and pretend to be the disciples. Choose one child to portray Peter. Set the mood for the story by saying, "Think about how scared you would be if you were all alone at night in a boat on the lake. The wind is blowing and the waves are crashing against the sides of the boat. It's so dark you cannot see ahead of you. As I tell the story, pretend to be the disciples and act like you think they did."

Tell the story. When the time is right, Jesus appears and talks to the disciples. Peter speaks, and Jesus reaches out a hand to help him across the water. The man playing Jesus can help the child across the water.

Have Jesus return to the boat with Peter. Let Jesus continue the lesson.

HINT

A cassette tape featuring blowing wind and raging water sounds really enhances this experience.

DISCUSSION

Have "Jesus" ask: "How did you feel when you were alone in the boat? Why? What could have happened? How did you feel when you saw me? Why?"

Ask the children if they have ever been in a terrifying situation. "What was it? Who helped you? Did you ask God for help?"

Remind the children that they are never completely alone. It is normal and okay to feel afraid when something scary is happening. Remind them that someone is always with them. Ask "Who is that?"

Children are fascinated by this story. "Can people really walk upon the water?" If you live in a climate that has cold, winter weather, remind the children that they have walked on water. "What is ice and snow?"

 A SONG TO SING

"Jesus Walked Upon the Water" by Cindy Dingwall
   (Sung to "Mary Had a Little Lamb")
Jesus walked upon the water, upon the water,
   upon the water.
Jesus walked upon the water.
What a miracle!

The disciples couldn't believe their eyes,
   believe their eyes, believe their eyes.
The disciples couldn't believe their eyes.
What a miracle!

Peter walked on water too, water too, water too.
Peter walked on water too.
What a miracle!

Ages 3-12

MATERIALS

Precut patterns for the boat and Jesus (1 per child) (See Appendix page 179)
1 large piece (12" x 18") of light blue construction paper (1 per child)
Blue plastic food wrap
Blue crayons—in a variety of shades
Black crayons
Gray paper cut into cloud shape (1 per child)
Glue

PREPARATION

1. Precut the boat with the disciples and Jesus.
2. Precut pieces of blue plastic food wrap so they will fit across the bottom half of the paper.
3. Print the scripture text from Matthew 14:27 on each cloud.

DIRECTIONS

1. Give each child a piece of blue paper.
2. Have the children use different shades of blue crayons to color water on the bottom half of the paper and midnight blue and black crayons to color the sky. Help them glue the blue plastic food wrap to the bottom half of the paper. Have them glue the boat and Jesus to the picture so it looks as though the boat is in the water and Jesus is walking on the water; then glue the cloud with the scripture verse on the paper.

IDEA

See pages 23-24 for puzzles that accompany this story.

WEEK 4: JESUS CALMS THE STORM

Mark 4:35-41

Ages 3-12

Use the same boat you used from Week 3. Ask the man who portrayed Jesus last week to return for this week's lesson. The children will be in the boat, portraying the disciples. Use a recording of a thunderstorm during the telling of this story. Turn it off when Jesus calms the storm.

Tell the story. When the disciples begin to show fear, Jesus can awaken and speak his part. Let Jesus lead the discussion.

DISCUSSION

This is another favorite story for children. All of us have been in frightening thunderstorms. Share experiences of being in scary storms. "What happened? Did you ever see a beautiful rainbow after a storm? Did you notice how clean and new everything looks after a storm?"

Ask: "Has anyone ever been in a tornado or hurricane? Tell us about what happened? How did you feel? How did other people feel?"

Remind children that God is always with us when there is a storm. Sometimes the storm doesn't end right away, but it ends eventually. God never leaves us alone.

SOMETHING EXTRA

Let "Jesus" read these stories to the children. He can say "I always enjoyed telling stories to people, especially to children just like you."

Stories to share:

Tyler Toad and the Thunder by Robert Crowe
There was a clap of thunder. Tyler Toad was terrified and hid.

The Storm Book by Charlotte Zolotow
Thunder crashed, lightning streaked across the sky and the rain pelted down. Then it was quiet, and a beautiful rainbow arced across the sky.

Talk about how the characters in each story coped with their fear. "What can we do when we are afraid?"

A Song to Sing:

"Jesus Stills the Storm" found in *Piggyback Songs in Praise of Jesus* compiled by Jean Warren.

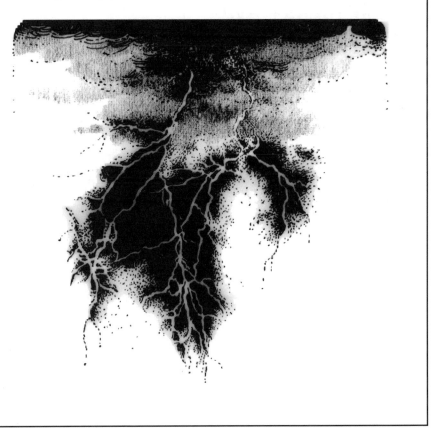

ART PROJECT: JESUS IS ALWAYS WITH ME

Ages 3-12

✂ MATERIALS

One large sheet of white construction paper per child (12" x 18")
Black, gray, and yellow crayons (for storm)
Assorted colors of crayons (for Jesus)
White glue that dries clear (one bottle per child)
Picture of Jesus
Piece of gray paper cut into cloud shape (1 per child)

📝 PREPARATION

Write on each cloud the words that Jesus speaks from Mark 4:39-40.

➡ DIRECTIONS

1. Have the children use the black and gray crayons to cover the paper with a storm. Yellow may be used to make lightning.
2. Pass out other crayons, and let the children color Jesus. Have them cut out Jesus and glue him to the center of the paper; add the cloud.
3. Children can use white glue to make raindrops. Lightly brush tip of glue bottle across the paper using very short downward strokes. When the glue dries, it will look like rain.

✖ VARIATIONS

Ages 6-12

▲ Write stories and poems about scary storms. Each story should show how Jesus helps us when we are afraid. These can be true or make-believe stories. Illustrate the stories. Add a cover and back page. Staple together to make a book.

▲ If there has been a recent natural disaster (for example, hurricane or tornado) help the victims in some way. Collect clothing, household goods, toys, books, puzzles, or money that can be sent to the relief centers.

💡 IDEA

See pages 24-25 for puzzles that accompany this story.

WEEK 5: JESUS RAISES LAZARUS FROM DEATH

John 11:1-44

Ages 3-12

Make a flannel board of this story. Tell the story using the flannel board pieces.

Show the children a living, but very thirsty, plant. Ask: "Why do you think the plant is dying? What can we do to help this plant?" Give the plant some water, and set it aside. By the end of class it should start to perk up. Talk to the children about drinking in God's word. "We need to learn about God's word to feed our souls. We need to eat food and drink water so our bodies will live."

DISCUSSION

Talk about miracles of people living even after the doctors thought there was no hope. Discuss what happens when people we love die. "They continue to live through our memories. We continue to love them." Remind children that when we die we will live in heaven with the Lord.

SOMETHING EXTRA

Stories to share:

The Dead Tree by Alvin Tresselt
   The tree had lived for years providing food, refuge, and shelter for many. One day it crashed to the ground. But it didn't really die, for it still provided food, refuge, shelter and new life.

The Giving Tree by Shel Silverstein
   The tree gave him everything she had, until there was nothing left for her to give. Even then she made a final offering.

A SONG TO SING

"Lazarus" by Cindy Dingwall
   (Sung to "Brahms Lullaby")
Lazarus was sick, and then he died.
All his friends and family; they were all very sad.
Jesus came to see his friend and learned that he'd died.
Jesus went to the tomb, and then he spoke,
"Lazarus arise and live once again,
For I am the Son of Eternal Life!"
Lazarus lived again and all were stunned.
There occurred a miracle of Jesus Christ.
Miracles, miracles, we give thanks for them all.
They're a gift from Christ who loves us all.

Ages 3-12

**MATERIALS**

1 glass baby food jar per child
Potting soil
1 package of lima beans
Small artificial flowers in spring colors (they should be on bendable stems)
1 12-inch square of fabric in spring colors or prints per child
1 12-inch long piece of colorful fabric ribbon per child
Spoons
Large bowl
Small watering can and water

PREPARATION

Empty bag of potting soil into large bowl.

DIRECTIONS

Use spoons to fill the jars with potting soil. Push 2 lima beans into the soil. Place jar in center of fabric square, pull edges up and tie with fabric ribbon. Water the plants. Remind the children to water their plants at home and put them in sunny place. In a few days their plants will begin to grow.

IDEA

See pages 26-27 for puzzles that accompany this story.

WEEK 6: PALM SUNDAY

Matthew 21:1-11; Mark 11:1-11; Luke 19:28-40; John 12:12-19

Ages 3-12

Make a flannel board of this story. Tell the story using the flannel board.

Give each child a palm branch. Explain that waving palm branches was a way of welcoming Jesus Christ. The green leaves symbolize hope and new life. Many years ago, people believed that trees and plants had a magical power that made them turn green in the spring. Touching a person with a palm branch was meant to bring them good health and good luck.

Discussion

Talk about why people were happy Jesus had arrived. Ask "How would you have felt if you had been there?"

Dramatic Play

Let the children act out the story. Assign the parts of Jesus and two disciples. If you have a horse on a stick, use it for the part of the donkey. The rest of the children can be the crowd. Have them line the walls of the hallway shouting, "Hosanna! Blessed is he who comes in the name of the Lord!"

 **SOMETHING EXTRA**

Story to share:
Pancakes and Painted Eggs by Jean Chapman
It is important to share all three stories: "Palm Sunday," "The Prayer of the Donkey," and "It Is Said."

Songs to Sing:
"Palm Sunday" and "Ride into Jerusalem" found in the book *Piggyback Songs in Praise of Jesus*, compiled by Jean Warren.

IDEA

The children can sing these songs as part of their play.

ART PROJECT: PALM BRANCHES

Ages 3-12

 MATERIALS

1 palm branch per child (cut from dark brown, extra heavy poster board)
12 palm leaves per person (cut from bright green paper)
One black felt pen per person
Glue
Bibles
Patterns for branch and leaf (Appendix page 181)
Staples and stapler

PREPARATION

For younger children, write the things Jesus did on the palm leaves before class. Give each child a packet of leaves to glue onto the branch.

➡ DIRECTIONS

Give each person 12 leaves and a black felt pen. Talk about the things Jesus did. Write them down and post them. Let children copy them onto their leaves. Glue (or staple) leaves to the branches. If gluing, allow time to dry before waving them around.

HINT

You may need to use your Bibles.

 VARIATIONS

Ages 8-12

▲ Allow the children to look through their Bibles and then find words and phrases that describe Jesus. Have them write these words and phrases on leaves. Attach them to a branch. Each child's palm branch will then be unique.

▲ Put leaves on both sides of the branches. Challenge the children to find enough words and phrases for the additional leaves.

Ages 3-12

▲ Gather all of the children in your Sunday school program. Give each child a real palm branch. At the beginning or end of the worship service, have them enter the sanctuary by coming down the aisles. They can have a parade through the sanctuary shouting, "Hosanna! Blessed is he who comes in the name of the Lord!" Have them stop, and remain standing in the aisles. Each child can shout out something Jesus did. "Healed a blind man! Fed 5,000 people! Calmed a storm!" and so forth. When everyone has had a chance to speak shout, "Hosanna! Blessed is he who comes in the name of the Lord!"

💡 IDEA

See pages 28-29 for puzzles that accompany this story.

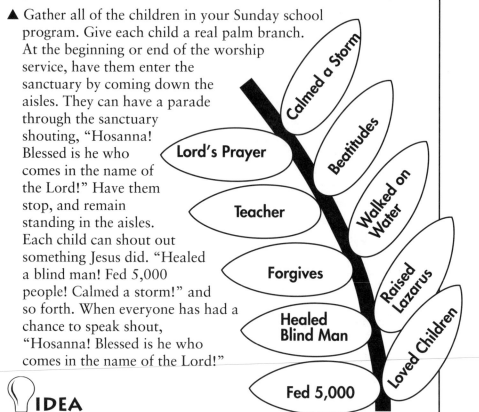

MAUNDY THURSDAY

Matthew 26:17-75; Mark 14:12-42; Luke 22:1-62; John 13:1-38

Ages 3-12

Provide a special "Time with the Children" to talk about betrayal during the Maundy Thursday service or at a special program. Betrayal is breaking a promise to someone. Give examples.

Have a group re-enact the Last Supper. Seeing this event acted out will help the children better understand what happened that night. Serve Holy Communion according to your church's traditions. Remind the children that Holy Communion gives us spiritual nourishment, giving us strength to carry on Christ's work. If your church allows children to receive Holy Communion, allow some of the older (8-12 year olds) children to assist by holding the loaf of bread and the cup while saying the appropriate words. See pages 131-32 for Agape Meal idea.

 A SONG TO SING

"The Last Supper" by Cindy Dingwall
    (Sung to "My Bonnie Lies Over the Ocean")
    Christ sat that night with disciples.
    Together they all shared a meal.
    He took some bread, and he broke it.
    And this is what he said,
    "Take this, eat this, do in remembrance of me, of me;
    Take this, eat this, for this is my body."

Christ sat that night with disciples.
Together they all shared a meal.
He took some wine, and he blessed it.
And this is what he said,
"Take this, drink this, do in remembrance of me, of me.
Take this, drink this, for this is my blood shed for you."

Talk about what happened that night during the meal when Jesus predicted his disciples would betray him. Tell the story of the disciples' betrayal.

 A SONG TO SING

"Peter Betrays Jesus" by Cindy Dingwall
    (Sung to "Rock-a-Bye Baby")
    Peter sat in the garden that night.
    He and the others were filled with fright.
    When they asked if he knew Christ,
    He replied, "I do not know that man!"

Just as Jesus said he would.
Peter denied that he knew him.
Three times he said the same thing.
And as he did, the rooster crowed.

SOMETHING EXTRA

Story to Share:
"Maundy Thursday" from the book **Pancakes and Painted Eggs** by Jean Chapman
    The story tells about the custom of washing feet.

ACTIVITY: WASHING OF THE FEET CEREMONY

Ages 3-12

Explain that roads in Jesus' time were made of dirt, and people's feet got dusty. When people arrived at other homes, servants washed their feet. Jesus showed he was willing to serve his disciples by washing their feet. "What are ways that we are willing to serve and help others?"

Have a tub of soapy water and some paper towels. Let the children take turns washing one another's feet.

ART PROJECT: _____, I WILL ALWAYS WALK BESIDE YOU

Ages 3-12

✂ MATERIALS

1 large piece (12" x 48") of white paper per child. This can be purchased in rolls, or tape several sheets of paper together.
Tempera paints
Paint brushes
Water
Paper towels
Soap
Chair
Newspaper

PREPARATION

1. Have a man make a set of footprints on each piece of paper. Paint the bottoms of his feet and have him walk along the right side of the paper. Allow to dry overnight.

2. Print the words: "I WILL ALWAYS WALK BESIDE YOU," _____ across the top of the paper. Leave a blank space at the left, so you can add the child's name before the phrase.

DIRECTIONS:

1. Cover the floor with lots of newspaper. Have a chair for the child to sit in. 2. Paint the bottoms of both feet (Use a different color than you used for "Jesus'" feet.) Help the child walk along the left side of the paper, so the smaller footprints are next to the large footprints. 3. Print the child's name on the paper. Let dry thoroughly. 4. Wash child's feet with soap and water. Dry feet with paper towels.

💡 IDEA

See page 29-30 for puzzles that accompany this story.

GOOD FRIDAY

Matthew 27:1-61; Mark 15:1-47; Luke 23:1-56; John 18:28–19:42

Ages 3-12

If possible include the children in your church's Good Friday service. Provide a "Time with the Children" for them where you show pictures and explain the crucifixion. Tell them that Christ knew that he had to die. He chose to die for us. Tell them how sad every one who knew him felt: his mother, his disciples, and others. Ask: "How do we feel knowing that Jesus died for us? How do you think we would feel if that were happening right this very minute?" Encourage the children to pretend they are at Calvary watching the events just as they occurred in the Bible.

Give each person two large nails when they enter the sanctuary on Good Friday. When it is time for the Crucifixion to occur in Scripture, each person may bring one nail up to put by the cross. The other nail is taken home to remind them of the Lord's sacrifice.

Have a large rock on the altar. Let the children see if they can move it. Make sure that it is heavy enough so they can't even budge it. Leave it there until Easter morning.

See page 131-32 for additional ideas.

VARIATION

Ages 3-12

Plan a special Good Friday service just for the children. Use the ideas listed above.

A SONG TO SING

"Crucifixion" by Cindy Dingwall
(Sung to "Clementine")

Jesus walked, Jesus walked, Jesus walked along the road.
Jesus walked, Jesus walked, Jesus walked along the road.
Walked to Calvary, walked to Calvary, with a cross upon his back.
Walked to Calvary, walked to Calvary, with a cross upon his back.
Hammered nails, hammered nails, into his hands and feet.
Hammered nails, hammered nails, into his hands and feet.
Placed a crown, placed a crown, of thorns upon his head.
Placed a crown, placed a crown, of thorns upon his head.
How he suffered, how he suffered, how he suffered for us all.
How he suffered, how he suffered, how he suffered for us all.
Then he died, then he died, then he died upon the cross.
Then he died, then he died, then he died upon the cross.
He was placed, he was placed, he was placed inside a tomb.
He was placed, he was placed, he was placed inside a tomb.
The world was dark, the world was dark, the world was very dark that day.
The world was dark, the world was dark, the world was very dark that day.

SOMETHING EXTRA

Stories to share:
The Tenth Good Thing About Barney by Judith Viorst
A little boy was comforted after the death of his pet cat when his mother encouraged him to think of ten good things about Barney.
I'll Always Love You by Hans Wilhelm
When his dog died, the little boy was comforted by the memory that he always told her he loved her.
Share the story:
"Calvary Robin" from the book **Pancakes and Painted Eggs** by Jean Chapman.
Jesus gave the robin a very special blessing.

ACTIVITY: I'LL ALWAYS LOVE JESUS

Ages 3-12

Talk to the children about all of the good things Jesus did. Think about what you have learned during Lent. Talk about the miracles. Show the palm branch you made on Palm Sunday, and discuss the things Jesus did to help us.

Remind the children it is important to tell God and Jesus how much we love them. They need to hear that from us every day. We also need to tell our families and friends we love them.

The children can write stories and poems about Jesus. Have them draw pictures to illustrate these. Bind them together to make a book that will go into the class, church or school library.

 **VARIATION**

Ages 3-12

Each child can create his or her own book to take home.

ART PROJECT: EYE OF GOD

Ages 6-12

MATERIALS

Two sticks per person
1 6" strand of solid colored yarn per person
1 3' strand of multicolored yarn per person
20 4" strands of solid color yarn per person
1 12" strand of multicolored yarn

DIRECTIONS

Tie the 6" strand of solid color yarn firmly, joining the sticks to make a cross. Wrap it around the sticks several times, and tie it off. Wrap the 3-foot multicolored yarn around the arms of the cross several times, looping it around each arm. Cut and tie it off. Make four tassels. Fold 4 strands of 4" yarn in half and tie at the top with a fifth strand. Attach one tassel at each end of the cross. Attach the 12" strand to the top so the "Eye of God" can be hung.

Tell children that the "Eye of God" can remind them that God watches over us *all* of the time. God knows where we are and what we are doing. That's how much the Lord loves us. Ask children to share their thoughts and feelings about knowing that God can always see us and is always watching over us.

HINT

Some children may find this frightening. Reassure them that God watches over us out of love and concern for us.

IDEA

See pages 31-32 for puzzles that accompany this story.

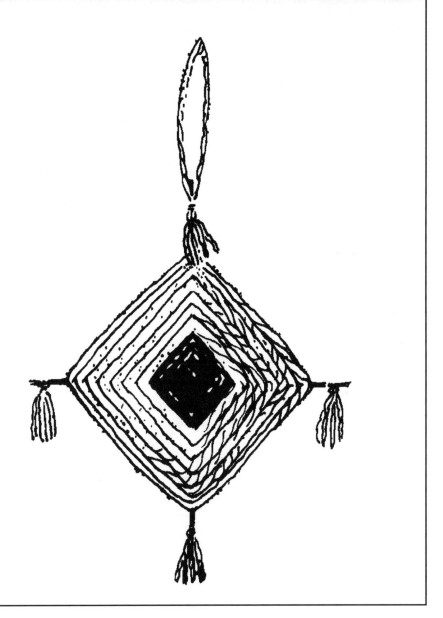

Matthew 28; Mark 16; Luke 24; John 20–21
Ages 3-12

Use story cards to tell the Easter story. Find a coloring book that contains the Easter story. Purchase two copies. Color the pictures, cut them out, and use rubber cement to attach them to cover stock paper. Write the appropriate text on the back of each card. Number the cards so you can keep them in the proper order.

Early Sunday morning, move the rock on the altar (see Good Friday) to a different location. Scatter flower petals on and around the rock. Ask the children to look around and see what is different from Good Friday. Show the children how the rock has been moved. "It moved! That big, heavy rock moved! How did it move?"

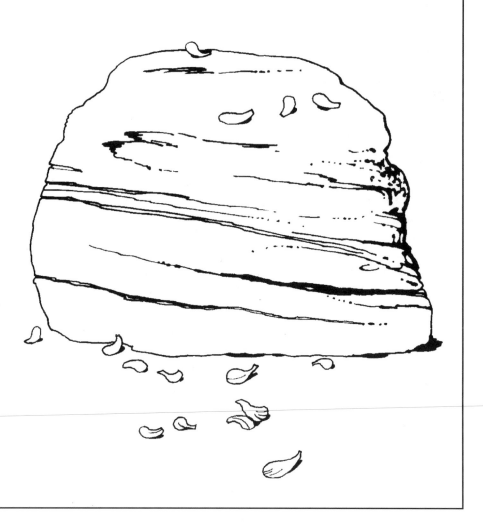 SOMETHING EXTRA

Use this book to tell the Easter story.
Easter by Jan Pienkowski
  Beautiful silhouette illustrations capture the essence of this story.

Songs to Sing:
  Sing any of the Easter songs found in the book: ***Piggyback Songs in Praise of Jesus*** compiled by Jean Warren.
A Story to share:
  Tell the story "Grandmother's Easter Flame" found in the book ***We Celebrate Easter*** by Bobbie Kalman.
Props: Large white candle on the altar
          Smaller white candle
  Light the small candle from the Easter candle. Carry it into the congregation and present it to someone.

ART PROJECT: EASTER CANDLES

Ages 3-12

✂ MATERIALS

One empty soup can per child (8 oz. size)
Enough play dough to fill each can
Candles (approximately 4" long by ½″ diameter)
One piece of pastel-colored paper cut to fit around outside of can.
Crayons
Markers
Tissue paper (cut into small pieces)
Glitter
Glue
Tape

DO AHEAD PREPARATION

1. Several days ahead of time, make the play dough according to the directions found on page 65.
2. Fill each can with play dough.
3. Insert a candle into the play dough. Put glue around the base of the candle to secure it in place.
4. Let dry for several days, making sure the candles stay upright and straight.

➡ DIRECTIONS

Give each child a piece of colored paper. Let them decorate the paper using crayons, markers, tissue paper and glitter. Attach the papers to the cans, taping the edges together. Take these candles to church members who are unable to attend Easter services.

✄ VARIATIONS

▲ Take the candle to a family member who is ill and unable to attend Easter services.
▲ Take the candle to a neighbor or family friend who is ill.

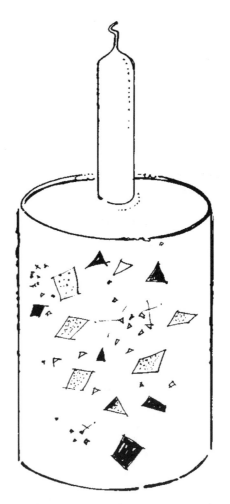

ART PROJECT: EASTER CROSSES

Ages 3-8

 MATERIALS

One brightly colored construction paper cross per child. (See Appendix page 182)
1 piece (12" x 18") construction paper per child
Colored tissue paper
Crayons
Glue

➡ DIRECTIONS

Have the children glue the cross in the center of the paper and decorate the paper with crayons and tissue paper.

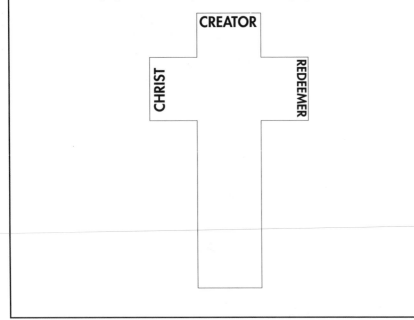

ART PROJECT: TELL ME ABOUT GOD (CHRIST) CROSSES

Ages 8-12

MATERIALS

3 crosses per person (precut from white construction paper) (See Appendix page 183)
1 large (12" x 18") piece construction paper per person

| Glue | Pencils | Bibles |
| Crayons | Tissue paper | |

DO AHEAD PREPARATION

Write: "Creator" on the top of the first cross
"Christ" on the top of the second cross
"Redeemer" on the top of the third cross

➡ DIRECTIONS

Have the children
▲ Use the Bibles to locate other adjectives for each cross. Write them on the appropriate cross.
▲ Glue the crosses to the paper.
▲ Decorate the paper with crayons and colored tissue paper.

ART PROJECT AND ACTIVITY: RESURRECTION CROSSES

Ages 3-12

✂ MATERIALS

Large pieces of foam core (available from craft stores) (1 piece per class)
1 48" x ½" dowel rod per class
Colorful ribbons
Colored tissue paper
Glue
Glitter
White paint
Brushes
Clear book tape (or white heavy duty tape)

PREPARATION

1. Cut board into crosses 3' x 2'.
2. Paint dowel rods white and let dry.
3. Attach dowel rods to back of crosses using heavy duty tape.
4. Make one cross per class.

➡ DIRECTIONS

Decorate the crosses using the ribbons, tissue paper, and glitter. Allow them to dry. Have the children carry these into the sanctuary during the Easter service or a special Easter program. Have some large potted plants on the altar or in the front of the room. Stick the dowel rods into the soil so the crosses stand straight. Keep them in the sanctuary or classroom for a couple of weeks after Easter.

HINT

Arrange this with your pastor ahead of time. However, keep your plans secret from other members. The congregation will be pleasantly surprised.

 A SONG TO SING

The children can sing this song as they carry the crosses.
"Christ Is Risen": by Cindy Dingwall
    (Sung to "Frere Jacques")
    Christ is risen!
    Christ is risen!
    Alleluia!
    Alleluia!
    Christ is risen!
    Christ is risen!
    Alleluia!
    Alleluia!
HINT: If using the song during worship, the congregation can sing along. Just signal them to begin. You can also sing it as a round.
    Ask your choir director to help with this.

IDEA

See page 32-33 for puzzles to accompany this story.

BULLETIN BOARD IDEAS AND GROUP ACTIVITIES

Good News! Even if you are not as artistic as you would like to be, you can create attractive, unique, and effective bulletin boards.

Enlist the assistance of everyone in your Christian Education program. Ask each class or age group to be responsible for a board one month. Allow the children to assist in their creation. If each teacher or group of teachers knows they only have to produce one per year, there won't be such a dread of doing them.

Use patterns from flannel board, coloring, and clip art books. Be innovative. Use different kinds of paper (corrugated, waxed, tissue, and so forth) and a variety of materials (felt, Pellon, fabrics, colored saran wrap, objects, and so forth).

This section includes three bulletin board ideas per month. Also included are instructions for completing the board, an illustration, patterns and a scripture. The scriptures can be used to highlight that month's programs.

The suggestions here are intended for the main bulletin board in your school, Sunday school, or meeting area. Use a board that is located in an area where it can be enjoyed by all who come to church or school. This is an excellent way to highlight your Christian education program.

You will need a large bulletin board. I have found that it is easier to work with an area of about 4' x 3' or larger. Feel free to enlarge or reduce patterns in this book (or in other books) to accommodate the size of your bulletin board.

Do not restrict yourself to the boundaries of the board. Be brave! Let parts of the display stray from the outside edges.

Group activities, projects, and events for each month are also included in this section. These can be used by parochial schools, day care classes, Sunday school classes, vacation bible schools, after-school programs, and clubs. The goals of these activities are to provide an avenue for sharing service projects and enjoying social events. Use the scripture lessons from the bulletin boards to highlight your activities.

Age recommendations are provided for each activity: ages 3-6 (preschool, kindergarten); ages 6-8 (grades 1-2); ages 8-12 (grades 3-6). There are many activities that are intended for all members of a child's family. These are noted with the designation "all ages."

Consider inviting all members of your church family to participate in these activities. It's fun to have programs that include a variety of ages and lifestyles.

SOMETHING EXTRA

This section includes stories that will enhance your programs. See page 67 for details of how to present stories.

The rest is up to you. Go forth, create and enjoy!

JANUARY: BLIZZARDS AND BLESSINGS

Title: A Blizzard of Blessings

Scripture: "All these blessings shall come upon you." (Deuteronomy 28:2)

MATERIALS

Dark blue paper

White paper circles (4 inches diameter) (Pattern, Appendix page 184)

Narrow strips of white paper (1" x 4") (Pattern, Appendix page 184)

Silver foil paper

Scissors, pencils, staples, glue

Camera and film for instant photos

DIRECTIONS

Background: Cover bulletin board with blue paper

Title: Using stencils trace title onto silver foil. Cut out title and staple to board

Snowflakes: Fold white circles into eighths, cut shapes out of the folded edges and open

Discuss: God makes each snowflake unique. No two are alike. God makes each person unique too. What blessings has God given us?

Blessings: Say: "Use the narrow strip of white paper to write a blessing God has given you." Attach the blessing paper to the snowflake.

Arrange: Attach snowflakes to the bulletin board by placing a staple in the middle of each one.

VARIATIONS

Title: A Blizzard of Blessings for the New Year

Scripture: "The faithful will abound with blessings." (Proverbs 28:20)

Take instant photos of the children, cut them into circles and glue in the center of each snowflake. Give each child's parents a strip of paper on which to write why their child is a blessing. Attach to snowflakes.

Title: (Church Name)'s Blizzard of Blessings

Scripture: "May your blessings be on your people!" (Psalm 3:8)

Candid photos of children and adults enjoying church activities together. Add a strip of paper with captions that explain each photo.

Talk about the miracle of snowflakes. Each snowflake, just like each of us, is unique. All of us are gifted in some way. Each individual has something special to share.

It is the beginning of a new year. Each year is filled with God's gifts, possibilities, and opportunities. How can we praise and glorify God in the coming year? Encourage your group to let this be a year to show our appreciation to God by concentrating on one talent (gift) (for example, spending more time reading the Bible, doing good deeds for others).

A New Year's Creation (all ages)

Children and their parents can work on this as a family. Each receives an 8" x 11" piece of blue paper folded in half and a white circle 4" in diameter. Make the white circle into a snowflake and attach it to the front of the blue booklet. Write down one thing you would like to accomplish in the coming year. Young children can draw a picture and dictate their thoughts. Tape the booklets shut. Take the booklets home, and attach them to the last page of your calendar. On December 31, open your booklet to see if you met your goal. As a variation families can decide what they would like to do as a family.

Birthday Book Club (all ages)

Set up a Birthday Book Club in your church. The proceeds go to purchase books for your church library.

Use foam core or heavy-duty poster board to design a large, decorated birthday cake. Display it on an empty wall where it will be easily seen. Invite members to join the Birthday Book Club during their birthday month. Add one candle to the cake for each member who joins the club. Write their name on the candle. Add the month and day of birth to the flame.

Provide a "wish list" that includes title, author, a brief summary, and the price of the book you would like to have for the library. You can also provide a selection of already-purchased books for people to choose from. Have the books ready for checkout.

Club members choose the book they want and pay for their selection. Paste a special "Birthday Book Club" donation plate with that person's name inside the book. Provide membership cards. Membership is good for one year and can be renewed annually by purchasing an additional book for the library. This project can be expanded to include audiovisual items.

A Winter Picnic (all ages)

Invite families to come to a Winter Picnic. Let the children serve as hosts. Since picnics are held outside, people will need to come dressed for the occasion. Those who live in cold wintry climates will need to dress for the cold, outdoor weather.

Spread large plastic sheets on the ground. Cover them with warm blankets and place large, plastic tablecloths over the blankets. If you live where it snows, having a picnic in the snow is great fun. To add to the enjoyment, have the picnic in the evening, and light the way with luminarias.

SOMETHING EXTRA

Read the story **The Winter Picnic** by Robert Welber
A boy convinces his mother that it is possible to have an outdoor winter picnic.

Eat picnic foods: hot dogs and hamburgers prepared on the

outdoor grill, peanut butter and jelly sandwiches, chips, fruit, cookies, juice, and other picnic foods.

After eating, engage in some wintry activities:

▲ Divide people into groups of 4-8 people to build snow people. See how many different ones you can construct and stretch along the front lawn. It may draw attention to your church and encourage people who drive by to visit your services.

▲ Make angels in the snow. If you don't remember how, ask a child to show you.

▲ If you have hills, go sledding.

▲ Go snowmobiling, cross country skiing, play noncompetitive games, have fun!

After frolicking in the snow for a while, everyone will probably be cold. Go inside for popcorn and hot chocolate. Watch a family film together.

Sandwich and Game Night (all ages)

This is a great family event for all ages.

Have people bring different kinds of breads and sandwich fixings (peanut butter, jelly, lunch meats, lettuce, tomatoes, cheeses, and so forth), chips, fruits, fresh-cut vegetables, and desserts. Supply beverages.

SOMETHING EXTRA

Share this story:

Sam's Sandwich by David Pelham

Sam created the most delectable sandwich ever!

Let everyone create their own sandwiches from the fixings provided.

Ask people to bring their favorite board game. Avoid video and electronic games. Spend an hour or two playing different games.

Conclude the evening by singing a few lively hymns that everyone knows.

Grandparents and Grandkids (all ages)

Contact a local retirement center about participating in some intergenerational activities with the children in your group. Many older people are without families, and many children live far from their grandparents. Meet with the activity staff of the retirement center to set up activities that children and older adults can enjoy together. Arrange for the residents to attend worship services or social events at your church. Take the children over to visit on a regular basis to establish an ongoing relationship.

Family Night at the Movies (all ages)

Choose a Christian film that is suitable for viewing by all ages. Invite children and parents to come and enjoy this film together. Enjoy popcorn and beverages. After the movie, take time to discuss it together. Encourage and allow the children to share their thoughts.

FEBRUARY: HEARTS FILLED WITH LOVE

Title: Our Hearts Are Filled with Love

Scripture: "I give you a new commandment, that you love one another." (John 13:34)

MATERIALS:

Black paper
Different shades of red and pink paper
Precut white hearts (one per child) (Pattern, Appendix page 185)
Camera and film for taking instant photos
Red foil paper
Letter stencils
Pencils, glue, staples, scissors

DIRECTIONS

Background: Cover bulletin board with black paper.

Title: Using stencils, trace title onto red foil. Cut out letters and attach to board.

Hearts: Have children cut hearts from the red and pink paper to create valentines. Encourage creativity and originality.

Discuss: How does God show love for us? How do we show love to God and other people?

Photos: Take instant photos of the children helping one another, showing friendship and love to others. Cut photos into circles and attach to the center of the white hearts.

Arrange: Tape the white hearts with photos to the wooden border of your bulletin board. Staple the valentines to the center of the board.

ALTERNATIVES

Title: Loving Hearts for God

Scripture: "You shall love the Lord your God with all your heart, and with all your soul, and with all your mind." (Matthew 22:37)

Take instant photos of each child, and cut them into circles. Give each child a white heart and let them glue their photo in the center. Tape these around the wooden border of the board. Use red and pink paper to make valentines for Jesus. Put these in the center of the board. (Feel free to reverse the placement of the white hearts and the valentines.)

Title: **Jesus' Heart Is Filled with Love**

Scripture: "Love one another as I have loved you." (John 15:12)

Have the children create red and pink valentines for Jesus. Tape these to the wooden border of the board. Make a large, red heart and place it in the center of the board. Take instant photos of the children, cut them into circles, and staple them inside red hearts.

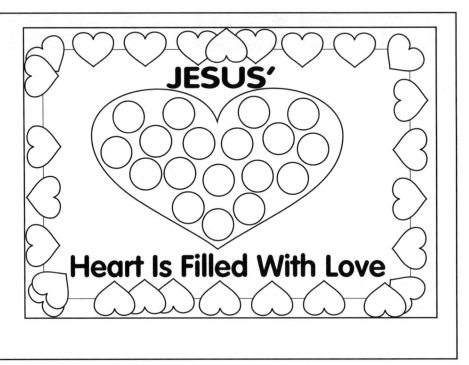

GROUP ACTIVITIES: FRIENDSHIP MONTH

Focus on the theme of friendship this month. Plan your activities and events so they include all members of your church school program or congregation. Invite friends to participate. Try to bring new people into your program or church.

Make Valentines (all ages)

Have each participant write his or her name on a pink index card. Shuffle the cards, then allow each person to draw a name from the stack. Without telling whose name was chosen, have each person create a valentine for the person on their card.

MATERIALS

Different shades of red and pink paper
White paper
Black paper
Scissors
Glue
Different shades of red and pink crayons
Pink and red pencils

DIRECTIONS

1. Cut out hearts and arrange them to make unique and interesting valentines.
2. Have people write a verse and sign their name.
3. Allow 20-30 minutes for everyone to finish.
4. Exchange valentines.
   You can also make and send valentines to:
▲ friends, relatives, or members who are home ill or hospitalized
▲ service men and women who are stationed away from home
▲ the children's wing of a local hospital
▲ the church Sunday school teachers, staff, choir members, church committees, and so forth
▲ area hospice center
▲ mental health wing of the hospital
▲ nursing home/retirement center
▲ make enough valentines for all the members of the congregation. Put them into large containers, and distribute them during the offering.

SOMETHING EXTRA

Share the story *A Friend Is Someone Who Likes You* by Joan Walsh Anglund.
Friends can be pets, people, or even trees.

Friendship Sundays (all ages)

Encourage children to bring a friend to Sunday school and church each Sunday during the month of February. Have special lessons on friendship.

We Miss You (all ages)

Make a special effort to get in touch with inactive members. Send "we missed you" postcards to children who are absent from Sunday school, choir, or your group.

Friendship Activities (all ages)

Encourage children to befriend a child who doesn't seem to have many friends.

Have an intergenerational Bible study on friendship. Learn what Jesus had to say about friendship.

Create a devotional booklet on friendship.

Help a friend who is experiencing difficulty.

Help the children in the church learn the value of friendship. Encourage parents to make February *Friendship Month* at home. Have them involve their families in activities that promote friendship. Encourage them to set aside 15-30 minutes each week during the month to explore this.

I Am Special! (ages 6-12)

Give the following directions to each participant:

On a blank sheet of paper write your first name vertically with one or more colored pencils. For each letter of your name, think of an adjective that describes you and is affirming. Remember that Jesus instructed us to love our neighbors as ourselves. Look up unfamiliar words in a dictionary.

C	reative	M	usical
A	rtistic	A	thletic
R	ollicking	T	alented
O	utstanding	T	raveler
L	oving	H	appy
Y	outhful	E	nergetic
N	ice	W	onderful

Decorate your papers.

Let's Show We Care (all ages)

Have a "cookie baking day." Ask parents and children to make a large batch of their favorite cookie dough, and bring it to church or class. Provide materials for cookie decorating, and decorate the cookies.

Put the cookies in attractive gift boxes, and take them to your local fire/paramedic department, police department, public works department, or library. Call the location you choose beforehand to find out how many people are on the staff so that you will have enough cookies for everyone. Deliver the cookies with a word of thanks for the service they provide. The children could prepare a song for their visit.

Title: March with the Lord and Sing!

Scripture: "Make a joyful noise to the Lord."
(Psalm 100:1)

Feature your children's choir this month.

 MATERIALS

White paper
Photos of the choir
   (One 8" x 10" of the choir, 4" x 6" candid photos of the choir rehearsing and singing during worship)
Red paper
Black paper
Red paper cut in 8½" x 10½" and 4½" x 6½" squares
Letter stencils
Scissors
Glue
A few pieces of choir music

 **DIRECTIONS**

Background: Cover bulletin board with white paper
Title: Use letter stencils to trace title onto red paper. Cut out title.
Music: Trace music symbols onto black paper (See Appendix page 186). Cut out and attach to board.
Photos: Take color photos of your choir rehearsing and presenting music during worship. Also, take photos of the directors, accompanists, volunteers, and so forth.
Arrange: Place lettering, photos, music symbols, and music on bulletin board.
Discuss: The ways music helps us worship.

ALTERNATIVES

Title: "March with the Lord"
Scripture: "And I will walk among you, and will be your God, and you shall be my people." (Leviticus 26:12)
   Cover the board with white paper. Ask a man with very large feet to make a set of footprints with red tempera paint on the white paper. Let dry, cut out, and attach to board. Ask the children to choose a color (for example, blue, green, orange and purple) for their footprints. Paint each child's feet, and let them make one set

of footprints on white paper. Let dry, cut out, and attach to board.

Title: "March and Sing for God!"

Scripture: "Come into his presence with singing." (Psalm 100:2)

Using the two ideas described above, attach the footprints so they appear to be walking across the board.

Many of these activities are devoted to Lent. Some will carry over into April for Easter.

Lenten Letters (ages 3-12)

Encourage your students each week during Lent to send a letter or card to a different friend. Recommend that they tell their friend how much the friendship means to them. At the end of Lent they will have shared their love with six friends. Work with young children and help them to choose or make a card with a picture and write a brief message.

Lenten Promises (ages 3-12)

Encourage your students to make a promise to do one thing each week or each day during Lent that will help someone else. They can help a friend, neighbor, or family member. Parents and children can work together to plan projects to do individually and as a family.

Murals of Love (ages 3-12)

Each week during Lent one class or group of children can create a mural to send to a friend, relative, or church member who is hospitalized or confined to a nursing home, care center, or their home. Make the mural colorful and fun. Ask a volunteer or the pastor to deliver it during a visit.

Lenten Crosses (all ages)

On the first Sunday of Lent, have a *Service of the Cross.* Coordinate the Scripture readings, sermon, music, and children's message. Invite parents, friends, and church members to attend.

Hold the service in a room large enough to set up tables and chairs. Offer a brief message, then pass out the materials listed below, and follow the directions.

MATERIALS:

1 large plastic bag
Brown play dough (recipe on page 65)
6 purple birthday cake candles
1 pink birthday candle
1 white birthday candle
1 piece of heavy-duty cardboard (8" x 10")

DIRECTIONS: Roll and mold play dough into a cross. Put it on the cardboard. Crosses should be 6" x 9".

Insert candles into dough. Mold dough around candles so they stay in place. The white candle goes into the center of the cross. The pink candle goes below it. Drip a small amount of glue around candles. Use the plastic bag to carry the cross home.

USING: Light the first purple candle on Ash Wednesday and the first Sunday, candle two on the second Sunday, and so forth. On Good Friday, light the pink candle. On Easter Sunday, light the white candle. Use the Lenten Devotional Booklet (see below) each time you light your cross.

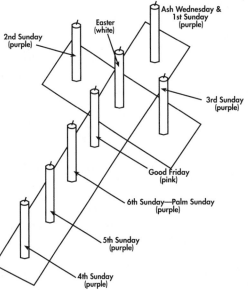

Lenten Devotional Booklet (all ages)

Prepare a Lenten Devotional Booklet for your congregation. Have one devotion for each day of Lent beginning with Ash Wednesday and ending with Easter. Include lighting ceremonies for Ash Wednesday, each Sunday in Lent, Palm Sunday, and Easter Sunday.

Devotions can include original songs, poems, psalms, prayers, or thoughts. Pair each devotion with a scripture verse. Begin collecting material early so that the book will be ready for Ash Wednesday. Give one to each family or individual.

Secret Pals (ages 3-12)

You will need a list of names, ages, grade levels, birth dates, and addresses of each child in your program (Sunday school class, day care/school class, group, and so forth). Invite adults to become Secret Pals to the children. Match one child to one adult.

During Lent, the adults will send messages to their Secret Pals. The messages can be birthday cards, postcards, notes, or an inexpensive surprise such as bookmarks, paperbacks, posters, candy bars, pencils, pins, and so forth. Act as a liaison between pals (for example, delivering a gift from a secret pal or delivering a message if a child wants to send a message to his or her adult pal.) Reveal the pals on Easter morning.

✦ HINT

Set guidelines for adults who want to prepare a special Easter surprise for their pal such as an Easter basket filled with goodies.

On the Sunday or during the week following Easter, have a party for the pals. Include stories, songs, games, and refreshments. Encourage the adults to keep in touch with their new friends. This is a wonderful way to bring children and adults together in friendship.

Lenten Study (all ages)

Develop a six-week intergenerational Lenten study for families. Include scripture, dramatizations, music, prayer, crafts, and special meals.

Title: God Gives Us New Life

Scripture: "See, I am making all things new."
(Revelation 21:5)

MATERIALS

Colored paper
Letter stencils
Scissors, glue, pencils
Staples, stapler
Push pins
Camera and film for instant photos
Yarn (various lengths)

DIRECTIONS

Background: Cover the bulletin board with any color paper.
  Multicolored paper would work well.
Title: Using letter stencils, trace title onto colored paper, cut out
  and attach to board.
Photos: Ask each child to bring a baby picture with his or her
  name on the back. Using rubber cement, attach each picture to
  a piece of colored paper, leaving a ½-inch border around the
  sides. Number each photo. (Make a list of "who's who.")
Arrange: Write each child's name on a separate piece of paper (1"
  x 6"). Staple these along the sides of the board. Use a push pin
  to attach a piece of yarn to each name. Put photos in center of
  board. Place a push pin under each photo.
  Children can try to guess "who's who" by attaching the yarn to
  the correct picture.

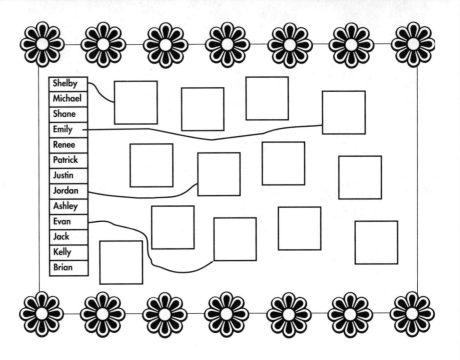

### VARIATIONS

Title: **God Creates New Life!**
Scripture: "So if anyone is in Christ, there is a new creation:
  everything old has passed away; see, everything has become
  new!" (2 Corinthians 5:17)
  Have animals hatching from eggs, baby animals with their mothers,
and pictures of new babies (in your congregation) with their families.

Title: Look Who's New

Scripture: "Greet the friends there, each by name." (3 John 1:15)
Cover the board with multicolored paper. Add colorful flowers. Display photos of children who are new to your Sunday school, class, or group. Include their names, where they came from, and a little about them.

Some of the activities you began in March will carry over into April.

The Great and Wonderful Candy Hunt (ages 3-12)

Organize an Easter Egg Hunt. Ask a class of older children to assist with the hunt. Include Easter stories and songs. Play noncompetitive games where *everyone* playing wins something (pencil, pin, bookmark).

Purchase (or have parents or members donate) individually wrapped candies. Hide these in the various church classrooms. Or if possible, hold this event outdoors. When hiding the goodies, keep in mind the ages of the children hunting. For the youngest children choose places easily spotted. For the oldest, make it more challenging.

Divide the children into groups by ages, and let them hunt for goodies. Provide paper lunch bags for children to use for their goodies. Have a special treat that each child receives (for example, bubbles, magnet, ball). These can be placed in the bags ahead of time.

A Basket Filled with Blessings (all ages)

Get the names of children in your congregation who will be hospitalized or confined to home for Easter. Prepare *A Basket Filled with Blessings* for each one.

 ### MATERIALS

One basket for each person
Easter grass
Ribbons
Fun activities: crayons, coloring book, paperback books, card

games, handheld games, book of word games
Food: fresh fruit, wrapped candy

 ### HINT

Provide age-appropriate activities.

 ### DIRECTIONS

Put the items into the basket. Tie the ribbon to the handle, and deliver the basket. Enclose a greeting card signed by the children in the class. Try to deliver it on or before Easter Sunday.

VARIATION (ALL AGES)

Make get-well cards from each child and fill the baskets with them.

Agape Meal (all ages)

Hold this event for children and parents on Maundy Thursday. Have families bring breads, fruits, and cheese. Provide juice for beverages. Host this event in the Fellowship Hall or large meeting area. Sing grace together for tonight's event.

On each table provide a variety of breads, fruit, cheese, and juice. Set each table to seat twelve people with one extra chair for Jesus. The pastor can go from table to table sharing Communion with each group. An alternative is to have a table for thirteen set up in a secluded place in your building (not the sanctuary). Each table of twelve will have a turn to go to the Communion table where the pastor will be waiting to share this time with them. Communion groups can be held while others are sharing the Agape Meal.

After the meal and Communion, go to the sanctuary and have a program about the Last Supper (dramatization, special music, children's story, and so forth).

Definition of Agape: This was a meal shared by early Christians. Originally it was combined with the Lord's Supper. It is a time to share Christian love for one another. *Agape* is the Greek word for love.

Scavenger Hunt (ages 3-12)

Organize a Scavenger Hunt. Divide children into teams of 4 to 6 members accompanied by one or two adults. Provide each group with a list of things to locate. Hide some of these on church property. For others, they may have to go to the store, the park, the library, homes of church members who live nearby, and so forth. For some items the children will need to rely on their creativity and imagination. Adult leaders of each group will need to have ideas for ways to assist the children.

Give each group a large paper bag and a list of 25-100 items to find (number depends on ages of children in each group). Make the list challenging, humorous, and fun. Vary the time they have to locate items in accordance with the age groups. Every team wins a prize (bookmarks, pencils, erasers, pins, and so forth). When the children return to church, feast on pizza and soft drinks.

Ideas for Items:

A church bulletin from another church, a cross, a newsletter from another church, a butterfly, a bookmark with a prayer or Bible verse, a Saint card, a church newsletter from your church, last Sunday's church bulletin (yours), a psalm, a prayer written by you, an original song, a dramatization of a Bible story, an original drawing of something God created, a photo of a new baby, a correct test paper (you provide the test with questions about your church, God and Jesus), a crossword puzzle (about your church, the Bible, and so forth), a pine cone, a blade of grass, a leaf, and so forth.

Baskets of Love (all ages)

Create an Easter basket for a child in need. Include age-appropriate items such as paperback books, toothpaste, toothbrush, stuffed animal, crayons, coloring book, toy, puzzle, and so forth. Give these to the local homeless shelter, a shelter for abused women and children, and so forth.

SOMETHING EXTRA

Share the story *The Tale of Three Trees* by Angela Elwell Hunt
Each of the trees wanted to do something special, and each of them did.

From Christmas to Easter Cross (all ages)

Make a wooden cross. Use waterproof paint to paint it white. With black waterproof write on the cross the words: "For the true meaning of Christmas, look to Easter." The children can carry this into the sanctuary on Easter Sunday. Save the cross to put in your church garden (see pages 135 and 148).

Title: God's Love Rains Upon Us

Scripture: God "covers the heavens with clouds, prepares rain for the earth, makes grass grow on the hills." (Psalm 147:8)

✂ MATERIALS

Cotton batting material used for stuffing (available in fabric stores)

Gray paper

Colored paper (pink, purple, red, orange)

Green paper

Yellow construction paper cut into circles (2 inches in diameter)

Pencils

Stapler/staples

Photos (school or instant) of each child

Green Easter grass

Clear cellophane strips of paper (they come cut as long, narrow streamers attached to a piece of cardboard)

Clear-drying white glue

Bright yellow paper

Letter stencils

Patterns for flowers, stems, circles, raindrops (Appendix page 187)

Background: Cover bulletin board with gray construction paper. Cover bottom portion of bulletin board with green paper cut to look like hills. Use Easter grass to create the grassy ground at the bottom of the board. Pull apart batting and arrange it to look like a large cloud. Tape cloud above the board. Keep the rain attached to the cardboard strip. Attach cardboard to the wall with heavy-duty tape so that it looks like the rain is coming from the cloud. (The cardboard portion should be hidden under the cloud.)

Title: Use letter stencils to trace the title onto yellow paper. Cut out and attach to board.

Flowers: Copy the flower patterns onto colored paper. Copy the stems with leaves onto green paper. Copy the circles onto yellow paper. Cut out shapes and give each child a flower, a yellow circle, and a stem with leaves. Glue these together. Glue the photo to the center of the flower.

Arrange: Attach the flowers to the bulletin board, so it looks like a colorful flower garden.

Discuss: God makes nature beautiful by giving us rain.

✕ VARIATIONS

Title: **God's Blessings Rain Upon Us**

Scripture: "Ask rain from the Lord in the season of the spring rain, from the Lord who makes the storm clouds, who gives showers of rain to you, the vegetation in the field to everyone." (Zechariah 10:1)

Cover the bulletin board with gray paper. Suspend the clouds from the ceiling just in front of bulletin board. Have rain streamers coming out of clouds. Cut raindrops from pieces of colored paper. Let each child write a blessing about the rain on each raindrop (flowers, trees, crops, grass, water for us to drink, lakes to swim in, oceans, and so forth).

Title: **God's Love Is in Bloom**

Scripture: "For as the earth brings forth its shoots, and as a garden causes what is sown in it to spring up, so the Lord God will cause righteousness and praise to spring up before all the nations." (Isaiah 61:11)

Cover bulletin board with blue paper. Copy the flower pattern onto different colored construction paper. Allow each child to choose a colored flower. Take instant photos of children (or use school photos) and cut them into a circle. Glue them in the center of the flower. Attach flowers to the bulletin board.

GROUP ACTIVITIES: SPRING PROMISES BLOSSOM

Concentrate on spring activities such as planting gardens, celebrating Mother's Day, and spring outings.

Garden Day (ages 6-12)

1. Have a garden day. Plant a variety of colorful flowers around your building. Include perennials and annuals. Set up a schedule of weeding and watering. Ask the children to sign up to do this for one week each during spring and summer.
2. Select an area that could become a church vegetable garden. Plant a variety of vegetables. When these are harvested, sell them. Donate the money to a local food pantry. Or donate the fresh vegetables to a local soup kitchen for the homeless.
3. Plant a pumpkin patch. Sell the pumpkins to raise money for special projects. See pages 152 and 153 for additional pumpkin ideas.

Team up children and adults to work together on creating your gardens. Put the *Christmas to Easter* cross in a special place in your garden. (See page 132 for instructions on making this cross.)

May Baskets (ages 3-12)

Make May Baskets to be taken to an area nursing home, convalescent home, or retirement center. Find out how many you will need so that each resident receives a basket. Or you may wish to give them to church members who are confined to home or hospitalized.

Fill baskets with unscented lotions, paperback books, puzzle books with pencils, magazines, and so forth.

Add colorful ribbons to the handle.

✗ VARIATION

Make "thinking of you" cards and drawings to put in the baskets.

Women's Sunday (ages 3-12)

Let the women and girls of the church lead a Sunday worship service. They can usher, serve communion, act as liturgists, offer the children's sermon, preach, and so forth. Have the women and girls from your choirs share an anthem written for female voices.

Do this on Mother's Day.

Spring Cleaning (ages 8-12)

On Saturday mornings in May schedule spring cleaning. Invite children and adults to sign up for one Saturday. The idea, of course, is to thoroughly clean every area of the school or church building. Have teams of people assigned to each room. Ask people to bring their own cleaning supplies and materials.

Serve breakfast to those who come to clean. Begin with an 8:00-8:45 prayer and breakfast time. Give out job assignments and clean from 9:00 to 12:00.

Garage Sale (all ages)

Ask families to do some "spring cleaning" at home and donate the items to the church or school. Concentrate on baby and children's clothes, baby equipment (cribs, high chairs, and so forth), toys, games, and puzzles. Items donated must be in excellent condition and have all of their pieces and parts. Have a garage sale of these items. Use the money for a special project or purchase for your children's programs, or donate it to an agency that serves children. Advertise your garage sale.

On the Greens (all ages)

Have a miniature golf outing. Let families and individuals sign up in teams of four players. Reserve space at a local miniature golf course for your group. Give a silly prize to each group who participates (highest number of shots per group, lowest number of shots per group, most creative golfer, and so forth). Go out for food after your tournament.

Moms and Kids Day (all ages)

Have a day where mothers and children come to a special program. Include stories about mothers and children, have a picnic lunch outdoors if possible, sing songs, play games, and create projects. See pages 35-66 for ideas. You could turn this into an overnight retreat.

Title: Set Sail with the Savior

Scripture: "Let us journey on our way, and I will go alongside you." (Genesis 33:12)

MATERIALS

Blue construction paper
Blue plastic food wrap
Navy blue construction paper
Red construction paper
Yellow construction paper
White construction paper
Scissors
Glue
White batting
Camera and film for taking instant photos
Letter stencils
Patterns of sailboat and sun (Appendix, page 188)
Pattern of Jesus (Appendix, page 179)
Staples, stapler

 ## DIRECTIONS

Background: Cover bulletin board with light blue paper. Put blue plastic wrap over lower portion of board so it looks like water.

Title: Use letter stencils to trace title onto navy blue construction paper. Cut out letters and arrange on board, or write the title on the sails and sailboat.

Clouds: Use batting to make the clouds. Put them in the sky.

Sun: Copy sun pattern onto yellow paper. Cut out and attach to board. (Pattern in Appendix, page 188.)

Sailboat: Enlarge the boat and sail patterns on a copier. Trace boat onto red paper and sail onto white paper. Cut out and glue together. Put sailboat into water so it looks as though it is sailing.

Photos: Photograph each child (upper body only). Cut the photo into an oval. Arrange the photos so it looks as though the children are sitting in the sailboat. Copy the pattern of Jesus found on Appendix page 179. Color him and put him in the boat with the children.

✂ VARIATIONS

Title: **Sailors for the Savior**
Scripture: "Take heart, it is I; do not be afraid." (Matthew 14:27)

   Cover the entire board with blue paper. Put blue plastic wrap over the entire background.

   Borrow a sailor's hat. Have each child pose for a photo wearing the hat. Cut around each photo so the child's head and shoulders are showing. Make one copy of the boat pattern per child (use a variety of colors). Attach each child's picture to the boat, so it looks as though the child is sailing it. Put Jesus into a larger boat in the center of the board. Use the pattern on page 179.

Title: **Sail the Seas with Jesus Christ**
Scripture: "And remember, I am with you always." (Matthew 28:20)

   Use the scene from "Sailing with the Savior," however eliminate the large boat for Christ. Using the Jesus pattern on page 179, cut out the top portion of Jesus. Give each child the picture of Christ's head and shoulders to color. Place the picture of Christ and a picture of each child into each sailboat.

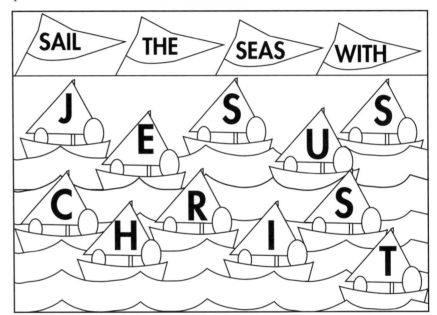

Celebrate summer with outdoor activities and events.

Help-a-Thon (ages 8-12)

Obtain a list of church members who need help with projects around their homes (cleaning, repairs, yard work, errands, and so forth). This would be especially helpful to those who are unable to do these jobs themselves.

Children and adults can work together on these projects. After they have completed their projects, encourage them to spend time visiting with the people they have helped.

Men's Sunday (all ages)

Have the men and boys in the church lead the entire worship service. They can usher, serve communion, offer a children's sermon, and so forth. Have the men and boys from your choirs present an anthem written for male voices. You can do this on Father's Day.

Sensational Summer Sundays (all ages)

Set up a series of *Sensational Summer Sundays* for members of your class or group and their families. Offer a variety of activities including worship services, picnics, social gatherings, and more.

Beach Blanket Worship (all ages)

"A Sensational Summer Sunday"

If you live near a body of water (lake or ocean), arrange to hold a worship service there. This would be an ideal time to do a baptism. Share the Bible stories about water (Creation—with a special emphasis on water, John the Baptist baptizes Jesus, water into wine at Cana, Jesus calms the storm, Jesus walks on water). Sing songs about water. Have a picnic afterwards. If possible engage in water sports (sailing, boating, water skiing, swimming).

Dads and Kids Day (all ages)

Have a day where fathers and children come to a special program. Include stories about fathers and children, have an outdoor picnic (weather permitting), sing songs, play games, and create projects. See pages 35-66 for ideas. You could turn this into an overnight retreat.

Title: Praise God for Our All-Star Kids

Scripture: "Let your light shine before others, so that they may see your good works and give glory to your Father in heaven." (Matthew 5:16)

 **MATERIALS**

Black construction paper
White cover stock paper (8½" x 5½")
White strips of paper (1" x 4")
Red foil paper
Camera and film for instant photos
Stars precut from cover stock paper
Glitter (silver, red, blue, green, multicolored)
Pencils
Glue
Letter stencils
Patterns for cards, star, circles (Appendix page 189-90)
String

DIRECTIONS

Background: Cover bulletin board with black paper.
Title: Trace title onto red foil. Cut out and attach to board.
Stars: Let children glitter stars using color of their choice.
Photos: Take an instant photo of each child.
All-Star Cards: Give each child a card to fill out. Glue photo in space provided. Attach star to top of card.
Arrange: Attach all-star cards to board.

Discuss: How each of us is special to God. God considers each of us "all-stars."

ALTERNATIVES

Title: **God's All-Star Kids**
Scripture: "Praise the Lord! . . . Praise God, sun and moon; praise God, all you shining stars!" (Psalm 148:1, 3 adapted)

Make the glitter stars. Take photos of the children and cut them into circles so they fit inside the stars. Glue photos to stars and attach them to the board. If you need more room, attach some stars to string and hang from ceiling in front of the board.

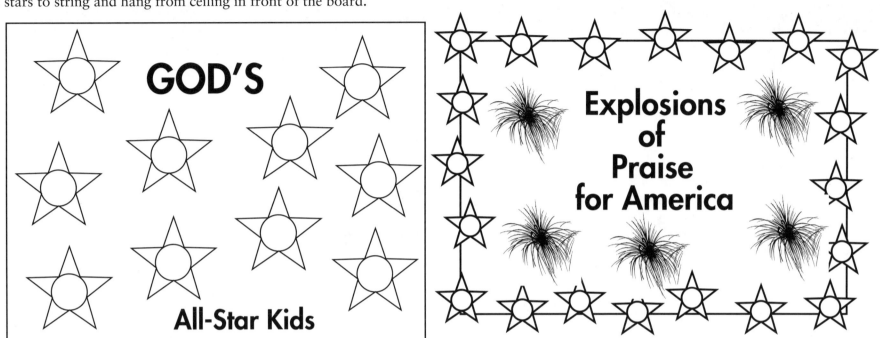

Title: Explosions of Praise for America

Scripture: "And the truth will make you free." (John 8:32)

Make the glitter stars. Take instant photos of each child, cut into a circle, and glue inside a star. Attach stars to outer edges of board. Give each child a black paper circle, glue, and glitter. Let each child use tip of glue bottle to draw fireworks on black circles. Sprinkle with glitter, and allow to dry. Give each child a strip of paper to write something they like about our country (freedom, mountains, oceans, school, and so forth). Attach each child's praise strip to their fireworks. Attach fireworks to the board.

GROUP ACTIVITIES: EXPLOSIONS OF PRAISE AND FUN!

Celebrate Independence Day with service and social activities.

Celebrate Freedom Packages (all ages)

Collect items that can be used by residents or patients in veteran or military hospitals in your area. Package them in an attractive container, and take them to one of these institutions. Contact the hospital you have in mind, and ask them what they need. The collected items might include: paperbacks, jigsaw puzzles, videos, audio cassettes, games, needlework kits, craft kits, handheld games, lotion, aftershave, and so forth).

Arrange a time to visit and deliver the materials you have collected. Include notes of appreciation to those who have served our country.

Outdoor Concerts (all ages)

Many communities have outdoor summer symphony concerts. Arrive early, to secure a spot close to where the symphony orchestra will perform. Enjoy a picnic lunch or dinner.

Host a summer concert on the church lawn. Invite instrumentalists from a local school (or use members of your church) and gather members of your children's choirs together to provide an evening concert of patriotic music. If desired, combine adult and children's choirs.

Bring blankets, lawn chairs, and a picnic lunch or dinner. Share stories about people who helped build our country. Admission is one of the following items: paperback adult book, jigsaw puzzle, craft kit, or other item suitable for inclusion in a "Celebrate Freedom" package.

Mountain Madness (all ages)
"A Sensational Summer Sunday"

If you live in or near the mountains, plan a Sunday worship service high atop a mountain. Ride the chair lifts or gondolas to the top of the mountain. Conduct a worship service that includes scripture readings about the mountains (Psalms 72 and 121). Include a children's story and sermon about God's glorious mountains. Sing "Climb Every Mountain" and "Go Tell It on the Mountain" with guitar accompaniment. Enjoy a picnic atop the mountain. Learn about the wild flowers and animals that live in the mountains.

After the service have a breakfast of fruits, breads, and juices. Enjoy a time of fellowship and games after breakfast. If there is a hiking path, spend the afternoon walking down the mountain. Allow those people who prefer to ride down.

America—Sweet Land of Liberty and Beauty (all ages)

"A Sensational Summer Sunday"

For the weekend of the Fourth of July, plan a special service that focuses on our country. Decorate your classroom or the church with the American flag, state flag, church flag, and so forth. You can also hang red, white, and blue bunting and garlands. Have scripture readings, special music, a children's sermon, and a special message about our American heritage. Sing patriotic hymns.

Plan a special event for after church or for that evening. Perhaps have your church picnic that day, or go as a group to view a local fireworks display. Eat foods that are red, white, and blue. Dress in patriotic colors of red, white, and blue.

Learn about America's famous children who have made important contributions to our country (President's children, Helen Keller, and so forth).

Clean America (ages 6-12)

Form teams of two to four people who will be assigned to canvas an area of your community. Have each person bring several large refuse bags. Each team will clean up the litter found in their area. The team with the most bags filled wins a special prize. Have an adult accompany each group.

Getting to Know You (all ages)

America is filled with individuals of different ethnic backgrounds. Host a special program where the different groups represented within your church or community can get to know one another better. Plan a meal that features foods from different countries. Teach songs, games, and dances from different cultures. Invite people to share interesting facts about their country or origin and how they celebrate their Independence Day. Encourage them to tell you how their families came to America. If possible, have them dress in their native dress.

Field Trip Fun (all ages)

Plan a trip to a local aquarium, zoo, or animal wildlife park. Learn about the animals you will see. Read about animals in the Bible. Talk about how and why God created animals. Decide what you can do as a community to protect the animals God has created for us.

Title: Soar to New Heights with God!

Scripture: "And the glory of the Lord has risen upon you." (Isaiah 60:1)

 **MATERIALS**

Blue construction paper
White batting
Colored construction paper (choose a variety of colors)
Markers and crayons
Yarn
Camera and film to take instant photos
Letter stencils
Pattern for balloon (Appendix page 191)

DIRECTIONS

Background: Cover the bulletin board with blue paper. Arrange batting to make clouds and attach them to the sky.
Title: Use letter stencils to trace letters on to various colors of construction paper. Cut out letters and attach them to the bulletin board.
Balloons: Make copies of the balloon pattern. Use a variety of colors. Let children use crayons to decorate balloons.
Photo: Take an instant photo of each child working on a balloon. Let each child glue his or her photo to the balloon.

 IDEA

An alternative is to take a photo of each family to place inside the balloon.
Arrange: Let children decide where to put their balloons on the board.

VARIATIONS

Title: Let Your Prayers Soar Up to God
Scripture: "Pray without ceasing." (1 Thessalonians 5:17)
Instead of putting photos on the balloons, have children write prayers on them. Prayers may include
▲ friends or relatives who are sick
▲ thanksgiving for teachers, parents, friends, and so forth
▲ praise for the good things that have happened
▲ activities and missions involving your class, church, or community
▲ personal concerns of the children (school, family situations, and so forth)

Title: **Let Us Soar with God**
Scripture: "I will ascend to the tops of the clouds." (Isaiah 14:14)
Showcase your children's activities and programming. Include photos of the children attending class and Sunday school, singing in the choir, and participating in church activities and community events.
Highlight the leaders and teachers who work with the children.

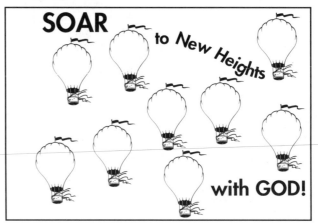

GROUP ACTIVITIES: SOAR TO NEW HEIGHTS WITH GOD!

Continue summer celebrations and begin to look forward to the start of a new school year.

Feed My Sheep Brunch (all ages)
"A Sensational Summer Sunday"

Have a "Feed My Sheep Brunch" after church that includes parents, friends, church members, and others. Allow the children to serve as hosts. Different children can introduce each course and read an appropriate scripture. Let the children create the prayers used. Talk about what Jesus meant when he said, "Feed my sheep."

Price of Admission: Each person donates one canned food item for the food pantry or food drive. Provide bushel baskets for donations.

During the games and activities section enjoy a time of fellowship and food. Have each class present something special (Puppet program, skit, songs, and so forth). Play the games "Match Makers" (page 42), "Praise God!" (page 43), and "A Picture Is Worth" (page 44) using scriptures about food.

If possible, picnic outdoors seated in circles on blankets. To divide people into groups, have them sit "alphabetically" (people whose first names begin with A, B, or C sit in one group; D, E, or F sit in another group, and so forth).

Welcome to Our "Feed My Sheep Brunch" (John 21:15-17)
Grace: (Let the children create this.)
Fruits and Juices: (John 15:5)
Breads: (Matthew 6:11)
Fish: (John 21:9-13)
Games & Activities
Benediction: (Matthew 14:20-21)

Sleep Overs (ages 6-12)

Schedule a series of sleep overs for children on Friday or Saturday nights. Invite a different age group each week. Have the adults who will work with each age group supervise those children at the sleep over. Divide sleep overs by age groupings (6-8 years; 8-10 years; 10-12 years). Use the games, puzzles and activities found on pages 35-51. Read and tell stories, act out Bible stories, sing songs, and watch videos. Tell just enough about the forthcoming Sunday school program to whet their appetites. Take time to talk about their feelings about starting a new school year. Share some of your school experiences with the children. Each child can be given a "party prize" (pencil, eraser, button, and so forth).

Price of admission:

Ages 6-8	(Box of crayons)
Ages 8-10	(Box of colored pencils)
Ages 10-12	(Package of #2 pencils with erasers)

Donate these items to families in need so their children have supplies for the new school year.

Happy New School Year Party (ages 3-6)

Have an afternoon program for children and their parents. Plan about two hours to enjoy games, activities, and refreshments. Take time to highlight the coming year. Each child can be given a "party prize" (button, pencil, and so forth). Price of admission: A bottle of school glue.

Back to School Paper Drive (ages 3-12)

Encourage children to donate packages of notebook paper, wireless tablets of paper, package of pocket folders, and assignment notebooks during the month of August. Put a large recycling bin in the school or church with an appropriate sign. Donate these supplies to an agency that works with families in need.

Take a Vacation (all ages)

Take a family vacation to the Holy Land with children and parents. Plan a week-long journey that begins on a Sunday evening and concludes the following Saturday evening. Each nightly program can last two hours. Make this an intergenerational program. Begin with a slide show of the Holy Land that you will view while "flying across the Atlantic Ocean." The flight is long and will take all of Sunday evening. Sing songs, talk about what you will do and see, have an onboard snack served on trays. Have your confirmation class members serve as flight attendants. The pilot can talk to your tour group, via the church public address system. Ask your high school youth group members to be the pilots and flight engineers.

Your tour begins upon arrival on Monday. Each night you will visit a different part of the Holy Land. Set up scenes that make your visit as realistic as possible.

Have some of your church members dress up to portray famous biblical characters who will tell you about their lives. Different characters can appear each night. On Wednesday night have a biblical treasure hunt where teams of people have a map and follow a set of clues to locate biblical artifacts. Each team will have to locate between one and five artifacts depending on the age group. Learn about each artifact.

Make related crafts, sing songs, and share appropriate snacks together.

On Friday evening have a "Fishes and Loaves" banquet. Begin with a brief introduction, play some games, partake in a delicious banquet, enjoy the entertainment, and conclude with a devotional.

On Saturday "fly" home. Enjoy an in-flight movie about Jesus. Have snacks. Talk about the film and the highlights of your trip.

Summer Showers (all ages)

Invite children and parents to participate in some "summer showers" where everyone brings a gift for a new baby. Include baby clothes, bottles, pacifiers, toys, lotion, soap, and other items babies need. Donate these to a center that works with parents and children in need. Set up a baby carriage or cradle so people will know where to place their donated items.

Title: Time for Sunday School

Scripture: "For it is time to seek the Lord." (Hosea 10:12)

 **MATERIALS**

Red construction paper
Black construction paper
White construction paper
Red construction paper circles (4" diameter)
Black markers
Brackets
Letter stencils
Glue
Patterns for clock (Appendix page 192)
Staples and stapler
Photos that highlight your Sunday school program (friendship, games, singing, stories, art, love, helping, puppets, drama, laughter, Bible, pictures of Jesus)

DIRECTIONS

Background: Cover the board with red paper.
Title: Use letter stencils to trace title onto black paper. Cut out and arrange on board.
Clock: Enlarge the clock and hands of the clock on a copier. The clock face will be white, and the hands will be black. Make 12 copies of the large circle on red paper. Make 12 copies of the smaller circle on white paper. Glue the white circles on top of the red circles so there is a red border around the white circles. Cut the photos into circles. Glue them in the center of the white circles. Write the appropriate caption under each photo.
Arrange: Arrange the circles so they are like the numbers that go around the inside of the clock. Attach clock hands using the bracket. Hands should be movable. Staple the clock to the bulletin board.
(Use this idea to highlight other programs as well: "Time for Vacation Bible School," "Time for Choir," and so forth.)

 **VARIATIONS**

Title: It's Time to Meet Your Teachers
Scripture: "Those who are taught the word must share in all good things with their teacher." (Galatians 6:6)
  Put photos of the Sunday school teachers inside the circles.

Title: It's Time to Learn About the Lord
Scripture: "The child grew and became strong, filled with wisdom; and the favor of God was upon him." (Luke 2:40)
  Inside the circles of the clock, put pictures of the Bible stories that the children will learn or various pictures of Jesus teaching others.

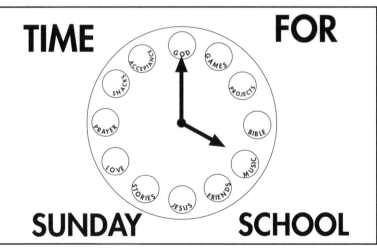

GROUP ACTIVITIES: TIME TO HARVEST AND SHARE GOD'S LOVE

This month's activities revolve around harvesting and sharing God's love with one another. Focus on the seeds of love we plant and nourish. When we harvest and share our love, it grows and grows forever.

An Autumn Harvest Dinner (all ages)

Have an Autumn Harvest Dinner for children and their families. Invite people to bring different autumn foods (for example, pumpkin bread, vegetable soup, apple cider, apple and pumpkin pies, popcorn, corn bread). Take the opportunity to highlight upcoming events you will sponsor for children and their families during the coming school year. Give each family a flyer listing these events.

SOMETHING EXTRA

Share the book *An Autumn Harvest* by Alvin Tresselt
In autumn we harvest all of the things we have planted and nurtured.

Seed Pictures (This can be part of your Autumn Harvest Dinner.)

MATERIALS

Heavy-duty poster board in different colors and sizes
Variety of seeds: (popcorn—regular and colored, sunflower, pumpkin, bean)
White glue
Pencils

DIRECTIONS

Use the seeds to make a picture of something God created. Lightly draw a picture with a pencil. Lay seeds on board, covering the lines you drew. Glue the seeds to the board. Dry flat overnight.

Hopes and Promises for Spring (ages 3-12)

Plant flowering bulbs around the school or church building. Talk about bulbs and about how they grow year after year. Choose a name for the garden and make a sign for it. You can put the "For the true meaning of Christmas, look to Easter" cross in the garden (page 132). Let parents know in advance, so children can come appropriately dressed. In the spring, use the flowers to adorn the church altar. Give each child a bulb to take home for planting.

Harvesting God's Promises (ages 3-12)

Begin harvesting the pumpkins from the seeds planted last spring. See the pumpkin activities in the October section on pages 152 and 153.

SOMETHING EXTRA

Story to share:
From Seed to Jack-O'-Lantern by Hannah Lyons Johnson
Learn how pumpkin seeds grow into pumpkins and become jack-o-lanterns.

Autumn Tree of Blessings (ages 3-12)

Bring in a large branch that has many smaller branches. Use plaster of Paris to secure this branch in a large pot. Provide precut autumn leaves made from yellow, red, orange, brown, and gold paper. Punch a hole in the top of each leaf and attach a piece of yarn that matches the leaf.

Invite the children to select a leaf, and with a marker, write something they like best about church or school. Hang the leaves on the tree. Keep the Autumn Tree of Blessings on display throughout autumn. Children may add one blessing per week if they desire.

Dinner on the Town (ages 6-12)

Set up a progressive dinner. However, rather than dining in people's homes, you will visit various eateries around town. Think of places children of your area enjoy eating (chicken, pizza, ice cream, and so forth). Are there any really unique places you could visit? Gather at church and proceed in order from one place to another. However, no one will be *told* just where it is they are to go. They must decipher a clue to get from one eatery to another. Envelope number 1 holds the first clue—perhaps a crossword puzzle that gives the name and address of the restaurant. All groups will proceed from place to place in the same order. All will dine at the same place at the same time.

As the group leaves the first place, the group receives envelope number 2 with the second clue—perhaps a puzzle they must assemble. The puzzle should include a picture of what they will eat, plus the name and address of where they are to go. As they arrive they will have to do something—maybe sing a song to get their food.

Envelope number 3 could contain a message that is written backwards and must be held up to the rearview mirror to be read. Be creative in your planning. Make it fun and enjoyable. Make advance arrangements with each place you are to visit. Before leaving the church or school call ahead to your first destination to let them know people will be arriving soon. Do the same with each additional destination. Preorder the food so it will be ready upon arrival. Charge a set fee for each individual who attends. Put children in groups of four to six according to the month in which they were born. Have one adult accompany each group.

OCTOBER: HARVEST AND SHARE GOD'S BLESSINGS

Title: Look at Our Harvest of Blessings!

Scripture: "Bless the Lord, O my soul, and all that is within me, bless his holy name." (Psalm 103:1)

 **MATERIALS**

Medium blue colored paper
Medium green colored paper
Light and dark brown paper
Orange paper
Yellow paper
Scissors, glue
Pencils
Letter stencils
Camera and film for taking instant photos
Patterns for leaves, bread, scarecrows, baskets, pumpkins (Appendix pages 193-194)
Staples, stapler

▶ DIRECTIONS

Background: Cover board with blue paper. Cover bottom part of board with green paper cut to look like hills. Put a sun in one corner. Put a large autumn tree on one side. Create an autumn scene on the bulletin board. Include pumpkins, scarecrows, and bushel baskets.

Title: Trace title onto yellow paper. Cut out and attach to board.

Photos: Take photos of the children (individually and in groups). Cut photos into circles and glue to the leaves.

Bread: Make one loaf of bread per child. Each child can write a

blessing they would like to share on their bread.

Arrange: Attach the leaves to the branches of the tree. Have some leaves floating through the air and others lying on the ground. Put the loaves of bread inside the baskets so you can see the blessings written on them.

✄ VARIATIONS

Title: **Bushels of Blessings!**

Scripture: "The faithful will abound with blessings." (Proverbs 28:20)

Use the autumn scene from above. Take photos of the children. Cut the photos into circles and attach them to the bread or leaves.

Have the children think of one word affirmations for one another. Explain that our good traits are blessings we can share with others. Write the affirmations on each child's leaf or loaf of bread. Include five affirmations per child (friendly, helpful, thoughtful, and so forth). Add these to the board.

BUSHELS OF BLESSINGS!

Title: **Harvest and Share**

Scripture: "And God is able to provide you with every blessing in abundance, so that by always having enough of everything, you may share abundantly in every good work." (2 Corinthians 9:8)

Use the same autumn scene. Include pictures of all of the children in your Sunday school or program. Place real bushel baskets under the bulletin board. Each Sunday, ask the children to bring one can, box, or package of nonperishable food as their weekly offering. Place these in the baskets below the bulletin board. By the end of the month your baskets will be overflowing. Take the items to a local food pantry and explain that they are a gift from the children of your church or group. If possible, take some of the children with you.

GROUP ACTIVITIES: "FESTIVALS OF FAITH AND FUN"

Focus on harvesting and sharing the blessings God has given us. What blessings do we have? How can we share them?

Pumpkin Festival (all ages)

Decorate the pumpkins you harvested (or let people bring their own). Be unique and creative. They can become famous people, Bible characters, animals, and so forth. Can you recreate a Bible story using pumpkins?

Hold a *Pumpkin Festival* for the community one weekend during the month. Charge a small admission fee. Feature storytelling, songs, games, and activities. Let people wander about and admire your creativity. Use this idea as a fund-raising activity. Also, provide information about your church, school, or program for visitors.

Scarecrow Festival (all ages)

Have family groups design and make a scarecrow. Everyone is responsible for securing their own materials and bringing them to the event. The church can supply the straw. Use newspapers for stuffing, and have the straw coming out of the arms, legs, and neck. The groups can create their scarecrows in the morning. In the afternoon have a festival where the scarecrows will be on display. Include storytelling with stories about scarecrows, sing songs about scarecrows, and have cider and taffy apples for snacks. Talk about how scarecrows are intended to help the farmer.

💡 IDEA

Combine the previous two ideas into a wonderful and fun *Scarecrow and Pumpkin Festival*.

Trick or Treat Food Drive (ages 3-12)

Instead of trick or treating for candy, have the children trick or treat for nonperishable food and personal items (canned goods, powdered potatoes, pasta, cookies, crackers, soups, bathroom and facial tissue, cotton, body lotions, soap, shampoo, and so forth).

Meet at the church wearing costumes. Have one adult for every two children five and under, one adult for every group of three to five children ages six to eight and nine to twelve. Each group of children will pull a wagon with them. Place one or two large boxes in each wagon.

Provide a typed list of food and personal items that are needed. Split the groups into various areas of the neighborhood so that the same people aren't visited by more than one or two groups. As the doors are opened, have the children respond with, "Trick or treat for food for the hungry." Explain your mission and present your list. Thank people for their donations.

Discourage people from giving candy with an explanation about the party with plenty of treats awaiting the children upon their return to the church.

When the children return, have the party. Divide into two groups: ages three to six and ages six to twelve can go to different rooms for age appropriate stories, songs, and games. Make sure all games played are noncompetitive, and that each child wins a prize for participating. Enjoy delicious goodies such as: pumpkin shaped cakes, candy, pumpkin cookies and cider. Give each child a small goodie bag with a few pieces of candy and a couple of party favors (pencil, bookmark, stickers).

On the following Sunday, have the children wheel their wagons filled with food to the altar during the time of offering. Explain to the congregation that this food will be given to a food pantry.

Pumpkin Fun (ages 3-12)

Gather the pumpkins you have harvested or purchase a few at the farm stand. Decorate the pumpkins and donate them to one of the following
▲ Children's unit at the local hospital
▲ Nursing home or retirement center
▲ Church members who are confined to home or hospital

Bake and Share (ages 3-12)

Call your local fire department to find out when Fire Prevention Week will be. Ask how many people work at each station. Spend a Saturday baking goodies (cookies, brownies, and so forth) to take to the fire departments that serve your community. Thank them for helping God keep us safe.

Title: God's Greatest Blessings Are Ours

Scripture: "May you be blessed by the LORD, who made heaven and earth." (Psalm 115:15)

MATERIALS

Orange or yellow burlap
Brown felt
Camera and film for taking instant photos (or use school photos)
Letter stencils
Brown construction paper
Scissors, glue, pencils
Pattern for cornucopia (Appendix page 195)
Staples, stapler

GOD'S Greatest Blessings Are Ours!

DIRECTIONS

Background: Cover the bulletin board with orange or yellow burlap. Create a large cornucopia from brown felt. Place on board.

Title: Use letter stencils to trace title onto brown paper. Cut out title and attach to board.

Photos: Take photos of all of the children. Use individual and/or group shots.

Arrange: Arrange photos so they spill out of the cornucopia.

Discuss: How can we be blessings?

VARIATIONS

Title: **Stuffed with God's Blessings**

Scripture: "Blessed are you who are hungry now, for you will be filled." (Luke 6:21)

Materials:

Bright orange burlap large enough to cover bulletin board
Large piece of brown felt
Yellow and red felt squares
Colored construction paper cut into feathers
Camera and film for taking instant photos (or use school photos)
Scissors
Black felt pens
Letter stencils
Patterns for turkey, feathers (Appendix page 195)

Cover the bulletin board with orange felt. Use a copier to enlarge turkey. Trace body onto brown felt, cut out and place on board. Use red and yellow felt to make features. Take instant photos of the children cut into circles and place them in the center of the body. Give each child a colored feather. Children can write blessings they give thanks for on the feathers. Let each child sign the feather. Attach the feathers to the turkey.

Stuffed With GOD's Blessings

Title: **Brimming with Blessings**

Scripture: "The blessings of the LORD be upon you!" (Psalm 129:8)

Combine the two ideas listed above into one bulletin board. You can have the photos of the children tumbling out of the cornucopia and feature their blessings on the feathers of the turkey. Another option is to put the photos of the children in the middle of the turkey's body, use real feathers for the turkey, and have the blessings written on fruit and vegetable cutouts flowing from the cornucopia.

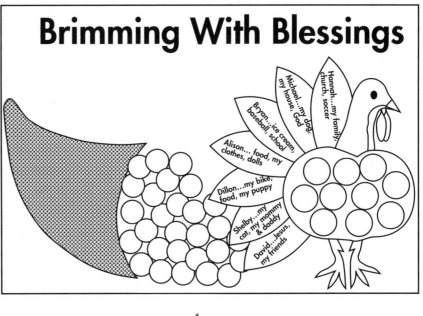

Brimming With Blessings

GROUP ACTIVITIES: "THANK YOU, GOD, FOR ALL YOUR BLESSINGS!"

Focus your activities this month on saying thank you for all of your blessings. Thank your family, friends, and God. Share your blessings with others.

Thank-You Notes (ages 3-12)

1. Have each child write a thank-you note to God. Let them share these with the group, if they desire. Younger children can draw pictures of what they are thankful for. During the morning offering, invite the children to come forward and place their thank-you notes on the altar.
2. Have the children draw pictures and write thank-you notes to your church staff: pastors, choir director (and choir), church secretary, custodians, and so forth. On the Sunday before Thanksgiving or at your Thanksgiving service, allow the children to present their notes to the church staff.
3. Using extra large pieces of construction paper, design large thank-you cards to be sent to various community helpers: fire department, police department, library, and so forth. Take some of the children with you as you deliver these notes.

Children's Book Week (ages 3-12)

Ask each child to donate a new book for this project. The book should be at that child's reading and interest level. Use a portable bookshelf for the donations. Make an attractive sign and place it above the shelf, so your display attracts attention. Encourage parents to help their children select hardcover books with outstanding stories and illustrations. At the end of the month donate these books to an agency or organization that serves children and their families in need.

Prayer of Thanksgiving (ages 3-12)

1. As a group write a Prayer of Thanksgiving. Ask your pastor if it would be possible to use this as a part of the worship service. Publish it in the church newsletter.
2. Have each child illustrate and write a prayer. Ask one of the children to design an attractive cover. Bind these together into a book. Add a blank back cover. Put the book in your church library.

Fill Me Up (ages 3-12)

Have the children make banks out of cans with plastic lids. Margarine tubs work well too. Each Sunday before and after church have the children approach the adults in the congregation and ask them to put change in their banks. Let them take their banks home and fill them with change during the week. Use a large container to collect the donations. Each week the children can dump their change into the container and start over with an empty bank. At the end of the month, total the amount the children have collected and donate the money to an organization that works with children, or purchase a much-needed item with their money and donate it.

Clean Out and Share (ages 3-12)

Have your children go through their toys, games, and puzzles and select one that they no longer use. These items *must* have all of their pieces, be clean, and be in excellent condition. Place a large toy box in the school lobby or near the altar. Ask children to bring donations during the month of November. At the end of the month donate them to a shelter that assists abused women and children.

Save and Share (ages 3-12)

Save all of the free samples of products you receive in the mail or in the grocery store. Use a grocery cart to collect the samples. You'll be surprised at how much you can collect. Encourage children to be responsible for collecting these items at home and bringing them to church or school each week.

An Afternoon on the Town (all ages)

Choose a puppet show, children's concert or musical to attend the Friday, Saturday, or Sunday afternoon following Thanksgiving. Purchase tickets in advance. Make reservations at a local pizza place for lunch. Go to lunch, then attend the performance. Charge a set fee that covers lunch and tickets. Consider renting a bus or van so everyone can travel together.

Title: Christmas Wishes and Stars

Scripture: "Arise, shine; for your light has come."
(Isaiah 60:1)

✂ MATERIALS

Dark blue, Green, Black construction paper
Silver cardboard
Camera, film for instant photos
Strips of paper
Patterns for tree, stars (Appendix page 196)
Scissors
Staples, stapler
Glue
Shiny red paper
Letter stencils
Red felt pens

➡ DIRECTIONS

Background: Cover the board with blue paper.
Title: Use letter stencils to trace title onto the shiny red paper. Cut out and attach to board.
Tree: Use a copier to enlarge Christmas tree (pattern on Appendix page 196). Trace tree onto green paper. Cut out and attach to board. Use black paper to make the trunk.
Photos: Take a photo of each child (or ask them to bring a school photo). Have each child attach their photo to the middle of a silver star.

👐 DISCUSS

What do we wish for at Christmas (for ourselves, our family, friends)? How can we show the Christmas spirit of sharing and giving?

Wishes: Encourage children to make a Christmas wish. Write the wishes on the paper strips and attach each child's wish to their star. Put the stars on the tree.

Christmas
Wishes
and
Stars

✕ VARIATIONS

Title: **Wishing on Christmas Stars**

Scripture: "The light shines in the darkness, and the darkness did not overcome it." (John 1:5)

Have a dark blue background with the green tree in the center. Cover the ground with white batting to resemble snow. Decorate the tree with small star stickers. Have the children make the glittery large stars. On one side attach the child's picture. Attach the child's wish on the other side of the star. Punch a hole in the top of each star, attach string and suspend the stars from the ceiling by the bulletin board.

Title: Our Christmas Stars

Scripture: "Praise him, all you shining stars!" (Psalm 148:3)

Cover the bulletin board with dark blue paper. Glitter the large Christmas star. Put a picture of Jesus in the center of it. Attach it to the center of the board. Have each child glitter a star. Place their photo in the center. Attach the stars to the board so they surround the Christ star. Tell the children about the extra special star that shone on Christmas Eve: "It was big and beautiful. It was different than all of the other stars. Why do you think it was different?"

GROUP ACTIVITIES: "WHAT CAN WE GIVE?"

Focus this month's activities on the gifts we can give to others and how to show appreciation for all the gifts God gives to us.

Three Gifts (ages 6-12)

Talk about the three gifts brought to Jesus by the three wise men. Give each child three cards—one red, one green, and one blue. These can be designed and run off on your copier. On the red card have the children write the gift they want to give to God (Jesus), on the green card have them write the gift they want to give to a friend, and on the blue card, have them write the gift they would like to receive. These gifts cannot be bought with money. Let them decorate their cards to look like presents. Have each person select one of their gifts to tell the group about.

Gift Bags (ages 3-12)

On the first Sunday of Advent give children and parents a paper bag with a list attached that will offer suggestions of filling their bag with gifts for a child in need. Perhaps people would like to decorate their bags or substitute an attractive gift bag. Invite people to fill their bags with gifts for a child in need.

Each list will designate BOY or GIRL and age of child. (Birth-2 years; 3-4 years, 5-7 years, 8-10 years, 11-13 years, 14-18 years). Items may include crayons, coloring books, balls, jacks, card games, paperback books, toothbrushes, toothpaste, hair ribbons, jewelry, small nonbreakable puzzles, books, school supplies, and so forth. For health reasons omit food and gum.

Have these returned to the church by the Sunday preceding Christmas. Let the children bring these to the altar during the offering. Distribute them to children in need in the community.

Stockings Filled with Good Wishes (ages 3-12)

Make up stockings for children who are confined to home or hospital during the holidays. Include paperback books, activity books, pencils, puzzles, games, and other items for quiet amusement. Make a card of good wishes from the children. Deliver these on Christmas Eve.

Variation

Fill the stockings with Christmas and get-well cards made by the children.

Mitten, Hat, and Scarf Tree (ages 3-12)

Set up an artificial tree in a prominent location. Invite children to fill it with scarves, hats, and mittens in all colors and sizes. Distribute these to people in need in your community.

Advent Devotional Booklet (ages 6-12)

Invite children to submit favorite poems, prayers, writings, and more for inclusion in this booklet. Include a special devotion for each of the four Sundays of Advent and a special devotion for both Christmas Eve (when the Christ candle is lit) and Christmas Day. Include devotions through Epiphany.

Advent Wreath Workshop (ages 3-12)

On the first Sunday of Advent, have an Advent Wreath Making Workshop. Have the service in the fellowship hall where you can set up tables and chairs. Have a brief worship service, and have the children's choir sing. Explain the history and significance of the Advent Wreath.

✂ MATERIALS

One green circular piece of craft foam per person
Three purple candles, one pink candle, and one fat free-standing white candle
Pieces of evergreen
One piece of heavy green poster board (14" x 14") per person

➡ DIRECTIONS

Place purple candles and pink candle evenly around the craft foam. Put wreath with candles onto the poster board. Set the white Christ candle in the center. Decorate with the evergreens. Give instructions on how to use the Advent Wreath. Provide copies of the Advent Devotional Booklet to use at home with the wreath.

Advent Calendar (ages 3-12)

Create a Church Advent Calendar. This will need to be large. Each space should be 12" x 12" so that there is room for each object.

Each day during the month of December add one symbol of Christmas. Include a brief typewritten explanation about each of the symbols.

End the calendar on January 6th, the arrival of the Three Kings.

Ideas for daily items are a variety of pictures and objects (manger, donkey, candle, star, cookies, and so forth). Try to include a mix of sacred and secular symbols. They all have special meaning that will enhance our appreciation of this time of year.

🎁 SOMETHING EXTRA

The book *Holly, Reindeer, and Colored Lights* by Edna Barth explains the meanings of Christmas symbols.

New Year's Eve Sleep Over (ages 6-12)

Host a sleep over. Parents may drop off their children beginning at 6:00 P.M. and pick them up the following morning by 8:00 A.M.

Each person should bring their own sleeping bag, pillow, toothbrush, and pj's.

Have several adults present to help. Parents must leave a phone number where they can be reached and sign a hospital emergency form giving you permission to seek emergency treatment until they can arrive.

Food:
1. Try a pizza-making party. Have premade crusts, cheese, tomato sauce, and a variety of toppings. Divide children into groups of four supervised by one adult. Let each person choose the topping he or she wants on the pieces of pizza.
2. Make and decorate cookies. Premix several batches of cookie dough, and let the children cut out shapes and decorate them. Eat them while they are still warm.

Games and Activities:
Read and tell stories, and have each pizza group act out a Bible story. Play some of the games in this book. Sing the songs from this book, or use the **Piggyback Songs in Praise of Jesus** or **Piggyback Songs in Praise of God** books.

Watch a movie: rent a good feature length film.

Art Projects: have a table where kids can create their own projects as well as a table where someone will teach them a particular craft or project.

At midnight welcome the New Year with prayers, praise, soft drinks, and popcorn.

Breakfast: How about a pancake breakfast for the parents and children?

A New Year's Creation (all ages)

Remember the snowflakes you created in January? Now is the time to open those cards and read about the talent you wanted to work on this year. Think about all you did this year, all that has happened, all you have learned. You will probably find you used your talent quite often. If you didn't do it this year but would like to for the coming year, read over the instructions on page 119.

APPENDIX

PUZZLE SOLUTIONS

Page 8: Sun—gives us warmth/light, helps things grow

Page 8: Rain, cloud, child, sun, fish, moon, star, dog, flower, tree, cat

Page 9: *Across:* 1. night   2. rested   3. birds
4. fourth
  Down: 1. animals   2. water   3. earth
4. God
  Message: It is good.

Page 9: Rainbow; It shined when the storm was over to remind us of God's love.

Page 10: Noah is located lower center

Page 10: *Across:* 1. Noah   2. animals   3. build
4. dove   5. water

Down: 1. rained   2. flood   3. hundred
Word: Rainbow; God loves us.

Page 11: 5 Angels

Page 11: Circles—Angels   Squares—Ladder
Ovals—Heaven   Rectangles—cloud; GOD

Page 12: I am with you and will watch over you wherever you go.
GOD

Page 12: Joseph's coat

Page 13: Joseph's coat

Page 13: Reuben, Simeon, Levi, Judah, Isaachar, Zebulun, Benjamin, Dan, Naphtali, Gad, Asher; Joseph's brothers; Jacob; their Father

Page 14: Mount Sinai (mountain)

Page 14: Moses

Page 15: Do not be jealous (10); Do not use bad words (3); Do not kill (6); Worship only God (1); Do not steal (8); Honor your parents (5); Do not lie (9); Honor marriage (7); Go to church on Sunday (4); Do not worship things (2); The Ten Commandments

Page 15/16: Whale that swallowed Jonah

Page 16: God forgives us

Page 17: Large star in middle is the Christmas star

Page 17: Follow the path

Page 18: Bethlehem; Jesus was born there

Page 18: Poor, heaven, blessed, comforted, meek, earth, hunger, filled, merciful, mercy, heart, God, peacemakers, children, righteousness, kingdom, heaven, you, me; Rejoice and be glad

Page 19: Triangles—Do; half circles—unto; circles—others; rectangles—as; diamonds—you; crescents—would; ovals—have; stars—them; hearts—do; squares—unto; blob—you; Do unto others as you would have them do unto you

Page 19: The Lord's Prayer

Page 20: Bread and fish

Page 20: Five loaves of bread, two fish

Page 21: Jesus feeds five thousand

Page 21: Hand

Page 22: *Across:* 1. leprosy 2. paralyzed 3. clean 4. demons

Down: 1. fever 2. blind 3. Jairus 4. bent over
Message: Miracles

Page 23: Circles—Jesus; squares—healed; ovals—many; rectangles—people; Jesus healed many people

Page 24: Jesus walks on water

Page 25: Jesus is upside down in the center.

Page 26: Jesus calms the storm (some words are scrambled)

Page 27: Lazarus

Page 27: I am the resurrection and the life.

Page 28: Donkey

Page 29: Donkey, Bethphage, blessed, Jesus, Nazareth

HOSANNA; It's what the people shouted when Jesus arrived on Palm Sunday.

Page 29: Wine/juice and bread

Page 30: Bread and wine/juice; They represent the body and blood of Christ. We have them for Holy Communion.

Page 30: The Last Supper

Page 31: Cross; Jesus died on it.

Page 32: Place of the Skull; Jesus was crucified here.

Page 32: The crucifixion and resurrection of Jesus

Page 33: Hearts—Christ; circles—is; triangles—risen; EASTER

Page 33: Cross, Jesus died on it, Joy appears twice, Good Friday goes in two directions

You will need to make a large flannel board for use in telling Bible stories. Each classroom needs to have its own board.

Making the Flannel Board

✂ MATERIALS

Large piece of plywood or heavy duty foam core. The board should measure 3 feet by 2 feet or larger.

Large piece of pale, neutral-colored (light gray or beige) Velcro hook and loop fasteners material. It should be large enough to cover both sides of the board.

Display stand capable of supporting the flannel board.

Flannel board material can be ordered from:

Charles Mayer Studios Inc.
168 E. Market St.
Akron, Ohio 44308

You can also order a ready-made flannel board from them. This product is well constructed and worth the one-time expense. It will last many years.

➡ DIRECTIONS

Use heavy duty glue (or a glue gun) to attach material to board. Another option is to have the material one inch larger than the board. Place two pieces of material together so that pieces are inside out. Use a sewing machine to stitch around two pieces of material using a ¼-inch seam. Leave one end open. Turn the material right side out, slip over board and hand stitch the opening shut.

Other materials:

Self-sticking Velcro in the following colors: *navy blue*, *white*, *beige*, and *red*. This can be purchased in fabric stores.
Felt in a variety of colors.
Several yards of white Pellon nonwoven textile. Avoid Pellon that is fleecy since it smears when coloring figures. This too can be purchased in fabric stores.

Making Flannel Board Figures

Pellon is good for creating flannel board figures. Place it over the picture and trace the picture onto the Pellon and color with crayons.

Cut out the figure and attach the rough side of Velcro to the back (a small piece will work). The Velcro sticks to the flannel board thus keeping the pieces from falling off. If you are unable to find self-stick Velcro, use a glue gun to attach Velcro to flannel board figures.

Be creative in your use of flannel board materials. Use animal prints and furs to make animals. Be willing to experiment with things such as angel hair, glitter, sequins, decorative borders, and more to add interest to your flannel board figures.

Resources for Creating Flannel Board Stories

Anderson, Paul S. *Storytelling with the Flannelboard.* Minneapolis, Minn: T. S. Dennison, 1963–1990. (3 volumes)

Darling, Kathy. *Holiday Hoopla: Flannel Board Fun.* Carthage, Ill. Monday Morning Books, Good Apple, 1990. May be ordered from: Good Apple, 1204 Buchanan St., P.O. Box 299, Carthage, Ill. 62321

Schneck, Susan. *Christian Clip and Copy Art.* Carthage, Ill.: Shining Star Publications, Good Apple Inc., 1989.

Sierra, Judy. *The Flannel Board Storytelling Book.* New York, Ill.: H. W. Wilson Co., 1987.

Taylor, Frances and Gloria G. Vaughn. *The Flannel Board Storybook.* Atlanta, Ga.: Humanics LTD., 1986.

Warren, Jean. *Mix and Match Series.* Everett, Wash.: Warren Publishing House, Inc. 1990. The four books in this series include patterns in four sizes. Includes animal patterns, everyday patterns, holiday patterns, nature patterns. May be ordered from: Warren Publishing House, Inc., P.O. Box 2250, Everett, Wash. 98203

Wilmes, Liz and Dick. *Felt Board Fun.* Elgin, Ill.: Building Blocks, 1984. Can be ordered from: Building Blocks, 3893 Brindlewood, Elgin, Ill. 60123

If you are interested in ordering ready-made flannel board versions of Bible stories, this company produces excellent products.

The Storyteller
308 E. 800 South
P.O. Box 921
Salem, Utah 84653

RESOURCES FOR STORYTELLING

Stories are suggested with several Bible learning lessons and monthly programs. Jesus was a storyteller and made good use of stories to highlight his teachings. We can continue that tradition in the church today. Each of the programs can be successfully used without these stories; however, the use of them will enhance the stories and provide an added dimension of enjoyment. Hearing a contemporary story that involves children will help youngsters understand and appreciate the truths taught in the Bible.

Check your local bookstore or library for these books and others that may be used in your programs.

Anglund, Joan Walsh. *A Friend Is Someone Who Likes You.* New York, N.Y.: Harcourt, Brace & World, 1958.

Baumann, Kurt. *The Story of Jonah.* New York, N.Y.: North-South, 1987.

Barth, Edna. *Holly, Reindeer, and Colored Lights.* New York, N.Y.: Seabury Press, 1971.

Bodker, Cecil. *Mary of Nazareth.* New York, N.Y.: Farrar, Straus, and Giroux, 1989.

Brent, Isabelle. *Noah's Ark.* Boston, Mass.: Little Brown. 1992.

Brown, Marcia. *Stone Soup.* New York, N.Y.: Scribner, 1947.

Carlson, Nancy. *Arnie and the Stolen Markers.* New York, N.Y.: Viking Kestrel, 1987.

Chapman, Jean. *Pancakes and Painted Eggs.* Chicago, Ill.: Children's Press International, 1983.

Crowe, Robert. *Tyler Toad and the Thunder.* New York, N.Y.: E. P. Dutton, 1980.

Elborn, Andrew. *Noah & the Ark & the Animals.* Natick, Mass.: Picture Book Studio USA, Alphabet Press, 1984.

Farber, Norma. *All Those Mothers at the Manger.* New York, N.Y.: Harper & Row, 1985.

Farber, Norma. *How the Hibernators Came to Bethlehem.* New York, N.Y.: Walker, 1980.

Fitch, Florence Mary. *A Book About God.* New York, N.Y.: Lothrop, Lee and Shepherd Co., 1953.

French, Fiona. *Rise and Shine.* Boston, Mass.: Little Brown & Co., 1989.

Gretz, Susanna. *Frog in the Middle.* New York, N.Y.: Four Winds Press, 1991.

Greaves, Margaret. *The Naming.* San Diego, Cal.: Gulliver Books, Harcourt Brace Jovanovich, 1993.

Hewitt, Kathryn. *King Midas and the Golden Touch.* San Diego, Cal.: Harcourt Brace Jovanovich, 1987.

Hickman, Martha Whitmore. *And God Created Squash.* Morton Grove, Ill.: Albert Whitman & Company, 1993.

Hunt, Angela Ewell. *The Tale of Three Trees.* Batavia, Ill.: Lion Publishing, 1989.

Hutton, Warwick. *Jonah and the Great Fish.* New York, N.Y.: Atheneum, 1984.

Johnson, Hannah Lyons. *From Seed to Jack-o'-Lantern.* New York, N.Y.: Lothrop, Lee and Shepherd Co., 1974.

Kalman, Bobbie. *We Celebrate Easter.* New York, N.Y.: Crabtree Publishing Company, 1985.

Lima, Carolyn W. *A to Zoo: Subject Access to Children's Picture Books.* New York, NY: Bowker, 1993 (periodically updated)

Malotte, Albert Hay. *Complete Lord's Prayers for Every Busy Accompanist.* Milwaukee, Wis.: G. S. Shirmer, Inc. 1990.

Pelham, David. *Sam's Sandwich.* New Mexico: Dutton Children's Books, 1990.

Pfister, Marcus. *The Christmas Star.* New York, N.Y.: North-South Books, 1993.

Pienkowski, Jan. *Christmas.* New York, N.Y.: Knopf, 1984.

Pienkiwski, Jan. *Easter.* New York, N.Y.: Knopf, 1989.

Rylant, Cynthia. *The Dreamer.* New York, N.Y.: Blue Sky Press, 1993.

Sharmat, Marjorie Weinman. *A Big Fat Enormous Lie.* New York, N.Y.: E. P. Dutton, 1978.

Silverstein, Shel. *The Giving Tree.* New York, N.Y.: Harper & Row, 1964.

Silverstein, Shel. *The Missing Piece.* New York, N.Y.: Harper & Row, 1976.

Singer, Isaac Bashevis. *Why Noah Chose the Dove.* New York, N.Y.: Farrar, Strauss, Giroux, 1973.

Sose, Bonnie. *Designed by God, So I Must Be Special.* Winter Park: Character Builders for Kids, 1988.

Spier, Peter. *The Book of Jonah.* Garden City, N.Y.: Doubleday & Company, Inc., 1985.

Spier, Peter. *Noah's Ark.* Garden City, N.Y.: Doubleday, 1977.

Simon, Henry W. *A Treasury of Christmas Songs and Carols.* Boston, Mass.: Houghton, Mifflin, 1973.

Tresselt, Alvin. *An Autumn Harvest.* New York, N.Y.: Lothrop, Lee and Shepherd Co., 1951.

Tresselt, Alvin. *The Dead Tree.* New York: N.Y.: Parents Magazine Press, 1972.

Tudor, Tasha. *Tasha Tudor's Favorite Christmas Carols.* New York, N.Y.: McKay, 1978.

Viorst, Judith. *I'll Fix Anthony.* New York, N.Y.: Harper & Row, 1969.

Viorst, Judith. *The Tenth Good Thing About Barney.* New York, N.Y.: Aladdin Books, Macmillan Publishing Co., 1971.

Warren, Jean. *Piggyback Songs in Praise of God.* Everett, Wash.: Warren Publishing House, 1986.

Warren, Jean. *Piggyback Songs in Praise of Jesus.* Everett, Wash.: Warren Publishing House, 1986.

Welber, Robert. *The Winter Picnic.* New York, N.Y.: Pantheon Books, 1970.

Wells, Rosemary. *Forest of Dreams.* New York, N.Y.: Dial Books for Young Readers, 1988.

Wilhelm, Hans. *I'll Always Love You.* New York, N.Y.: Dragonfly Books, Crown Publishers, 1985.

Wood, Audrey. *Elbert's Bad Word.* San Diego, Cal.: Harcourt Brace Jovanovich, 1988.

Wood, Douglas. *Old Turtle.* Duluth, Minn.: Pfeifer-Hamilton Publishers, 1992.

Zolotow, Charlotte. *Do You Know What I'll Do?* New York, N.Y.: Harper & Row, 1958.

Zolotow, Charlotte. *The Storm Book.* New York, N.Y.: Harper Collins, 1952.

CREATING BULLETIN BOARDS

1. Patterns can be enlarged or reduced on a copier.
2. Overhead projectors can be used to reproduce patterns. Tape a piece of white paper to the wall, beam the projected image onto the paper, and trace the picture.
3. Purchase several styles and sizes of alphabet stencils. Use the kind that have individually cut letters. Keep each set in its own envelope. Label backs of letters and envelope so each set stays together.
4. When tracing letters onto paper, lay each letter face down on the back of the paper, so it looks like you are tracing the letter backwards. When cut, visible pencil lines will be on the back of the letters.
5. Save your displays each year. Place them in large folders. Label the folder and have a list of what each folder contains.
6. Take a close-up color photo of each bulletin board. Have two copies made. Keep one with the folder and file the other in an album so you have a permanent record of each bulletin board.
7. Attractive borders for bulletin boards can be found in teacher supply stores.

SOMETHING SPECIAL

Have a place beside the bulletin board where you display the scripture verse of the month. Those children who memorize it and can tell you what it means in their own words can be awarded a prize.

January—Bookmark
February—Candy heart
March—Music sticker
April—Chocolate bunny
May—Scripture card
June—Flag
July—Scripture magnet
August—Pencil
September—Pencil topper
October—Scripture eraser
November—Scripture button
December—Candy cane

Avoid contests of who memorizes the most verses. The idea is to encourage children to enjoy memorizing scripture. Keep track of the children who participate for your own records, just in case some children try to win more than once a month.

PATTERNS

PATTERN FOR JONAH

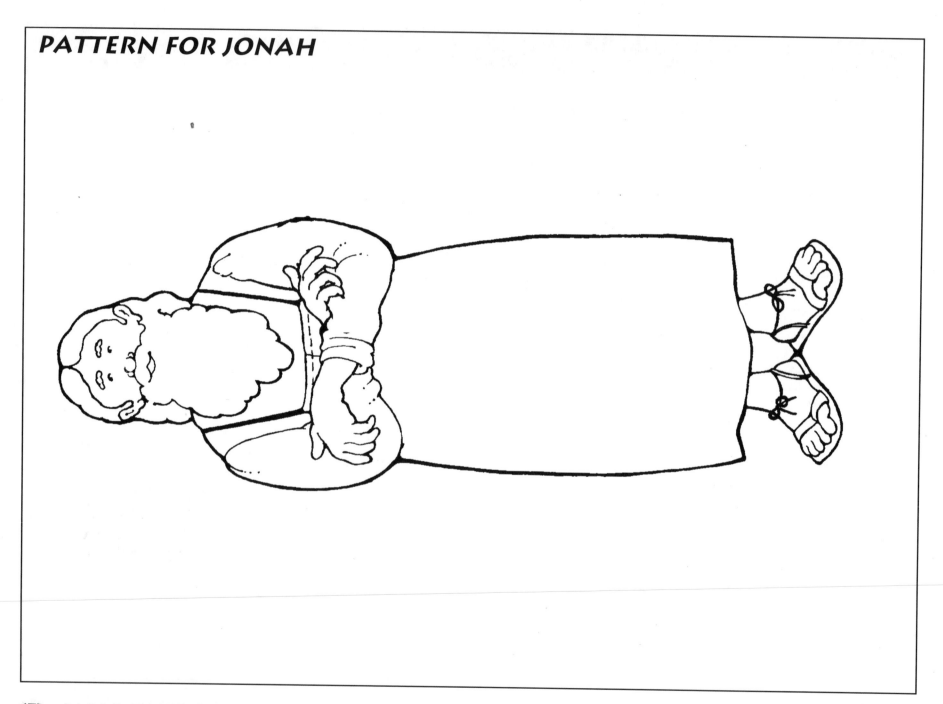

PATTERN FOR WHALE

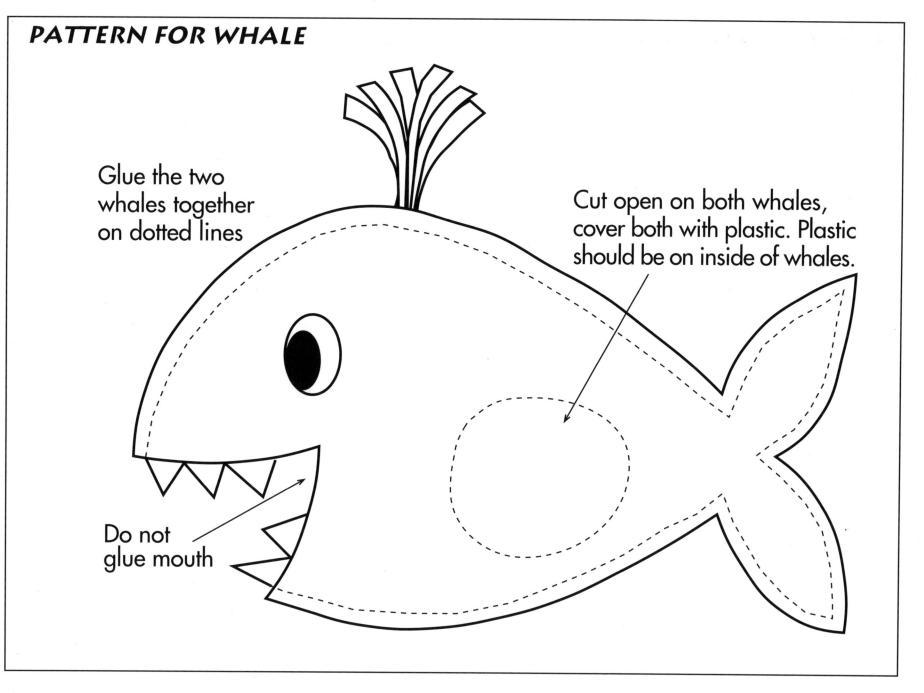

Glue the two whales together on dotted lines

Cut open on both whales, cover both with plastic. Plastic should be on inside of whales.

Do not glue mouth

PATTERN FOR FRAMES (CHRISTMAS STORY MURALS)

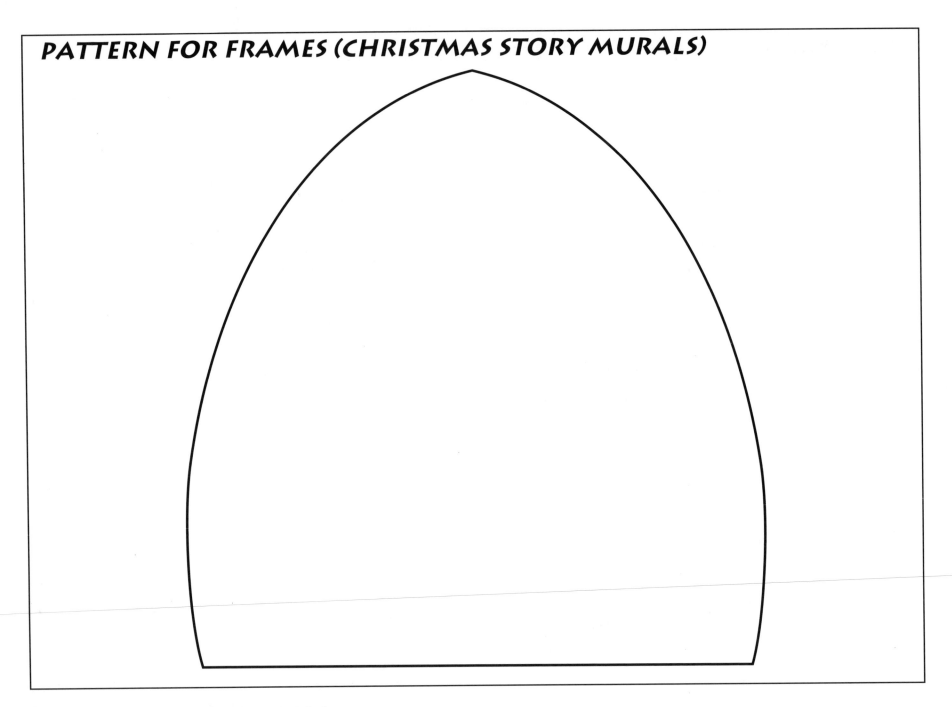

PATTERN FOR CIRCLES (CHRISTMAS RIBBONS)

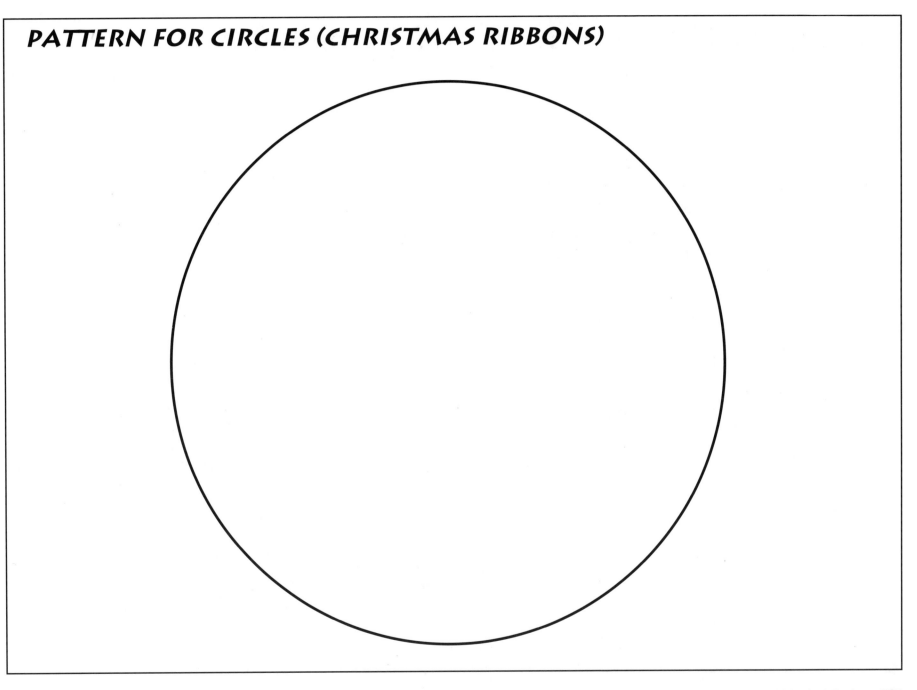

PATTERNS FOR PICTURES (CHRISTMAS STORY MURALS)

PATTERNS FOR PICTURES (CHRISTMAS STORY MURALS)

PATTERN FOR FISH

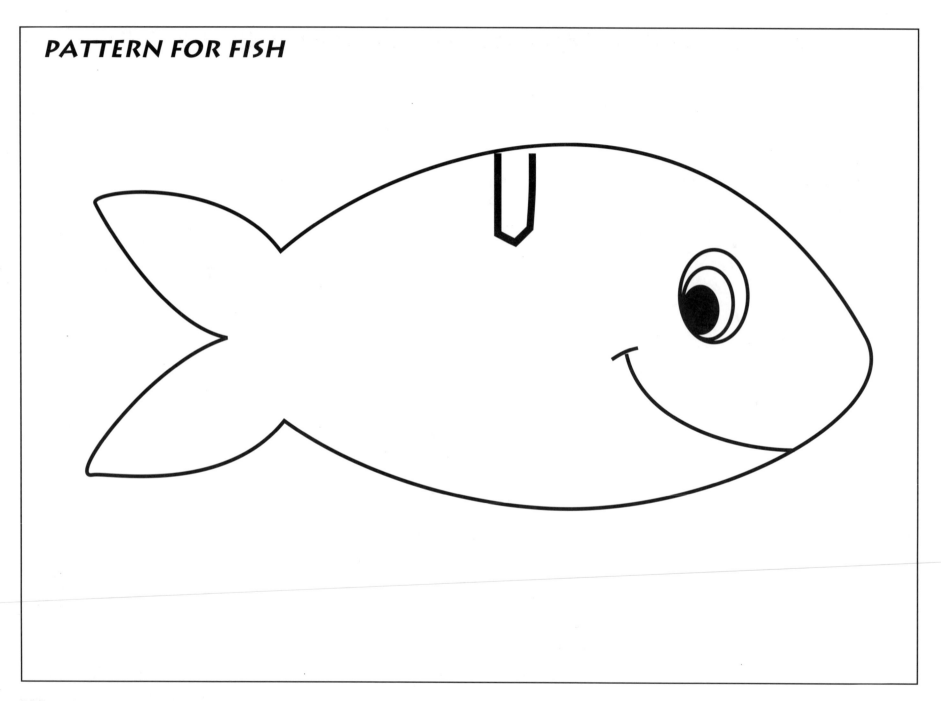

PATTERN FOR THE BOAT AND JESUS (JESUS WALKS ON WATER)

PATTERN FOR JESUS (JESUS CALMS THE STORM)

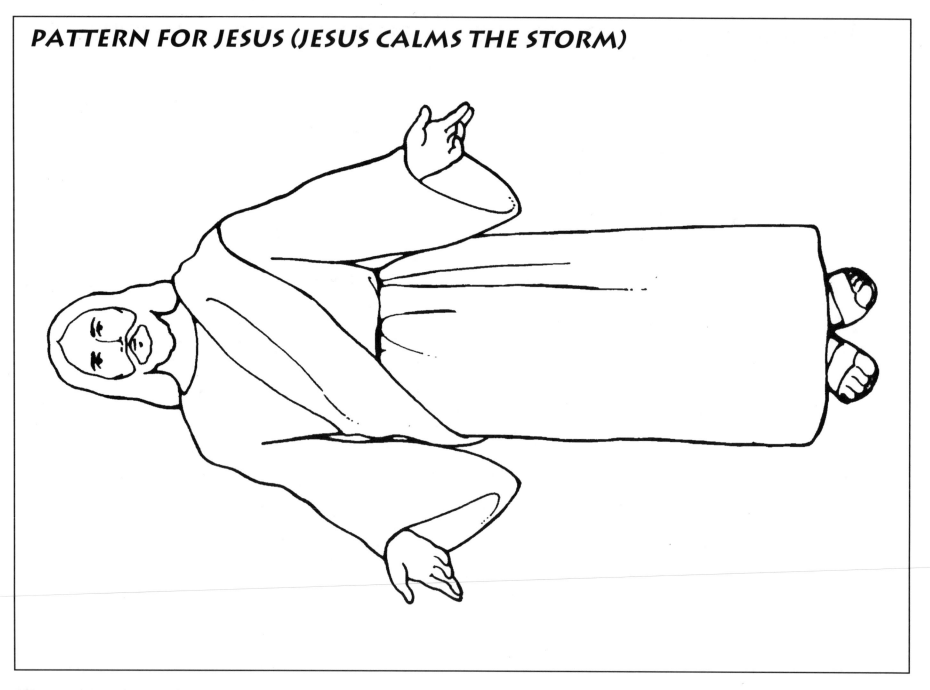

PATTERN FOR BRANCHES AND LEAVES (FOR PALM BRANCHES)

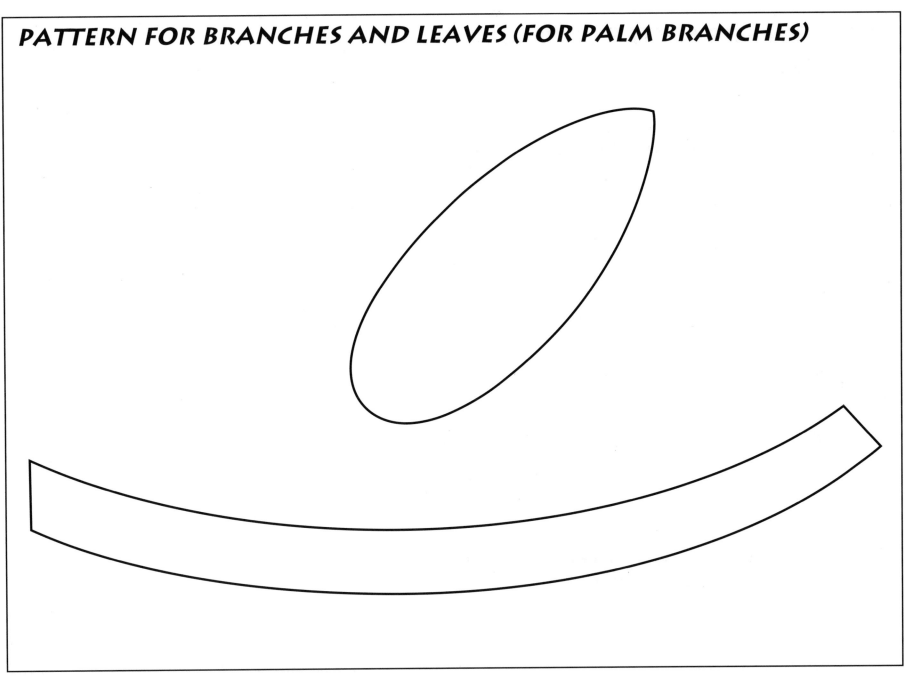

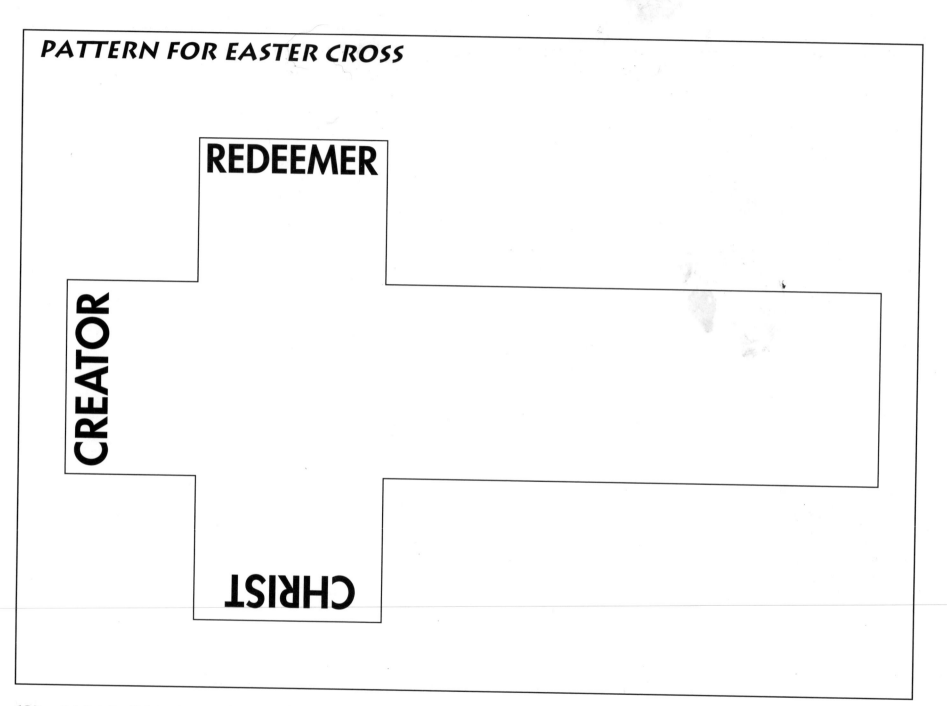

PATTERN FOR EASTER CROSS

REDEEMER

CREATOR

CHRIST

PATTERN FOR TELL ME ABOUT GOD CROSSES

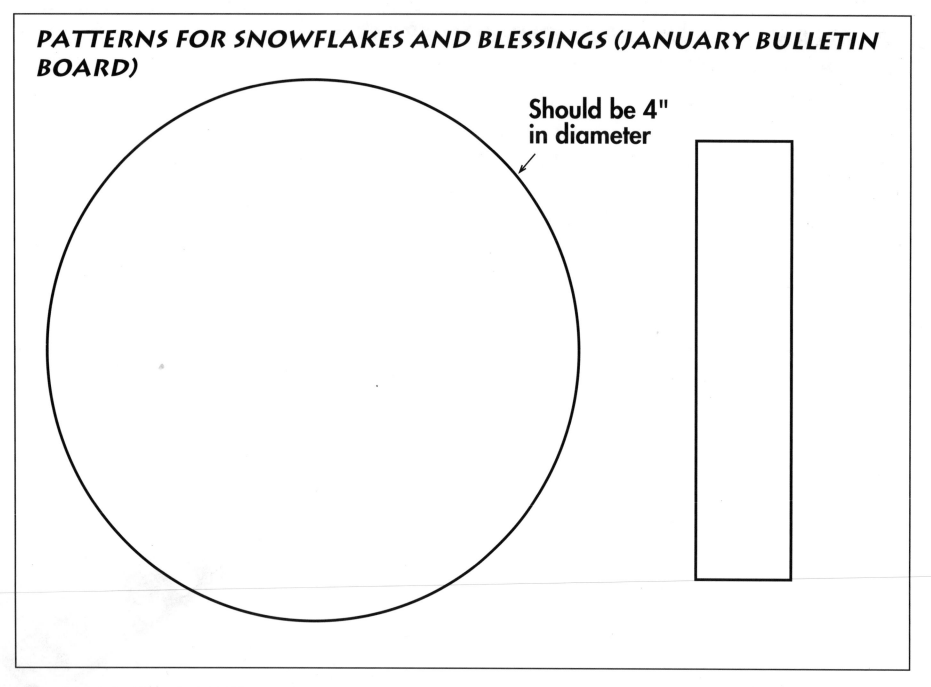

PATTERNS FOR SNOWFLAKES AND BLESSINGS (JANUARY BULLETIN BOARD)

Should be 4" in diameter

PATTERNS FOR WHITE HEARTS WITH PHOTOS (FEBRUARY BULLETIN BOARD)

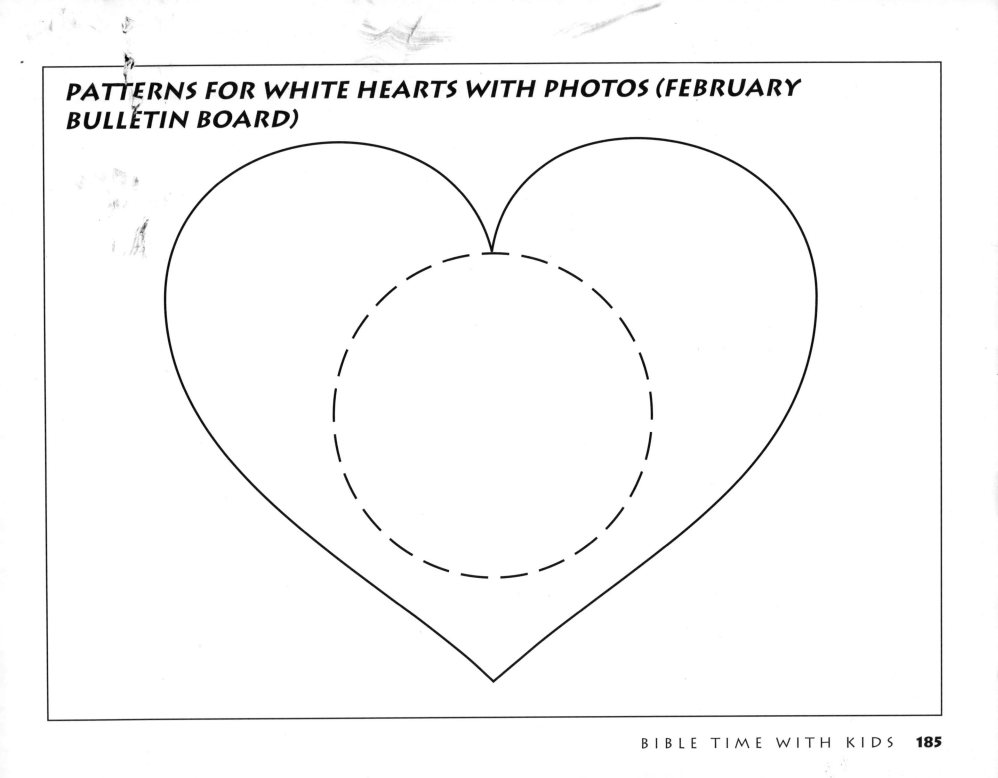

PATTERNS FOR MUSIC SYMBOLS (MARCH BULLETIN BOARD)

PATTERNS FOR FLOWERS, CIRCLES, STEMS, AND RAINDROPS (MAY BULLETIN BOARD)

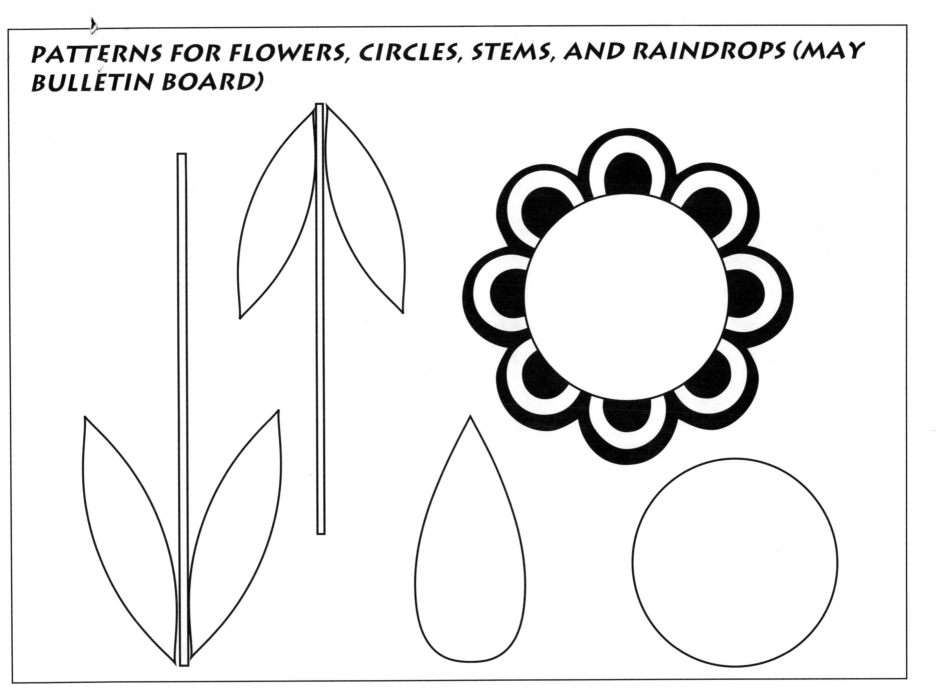

PATTERN FOR SAILBOAT AND SUN (JUNE BULLETIN BOARD)

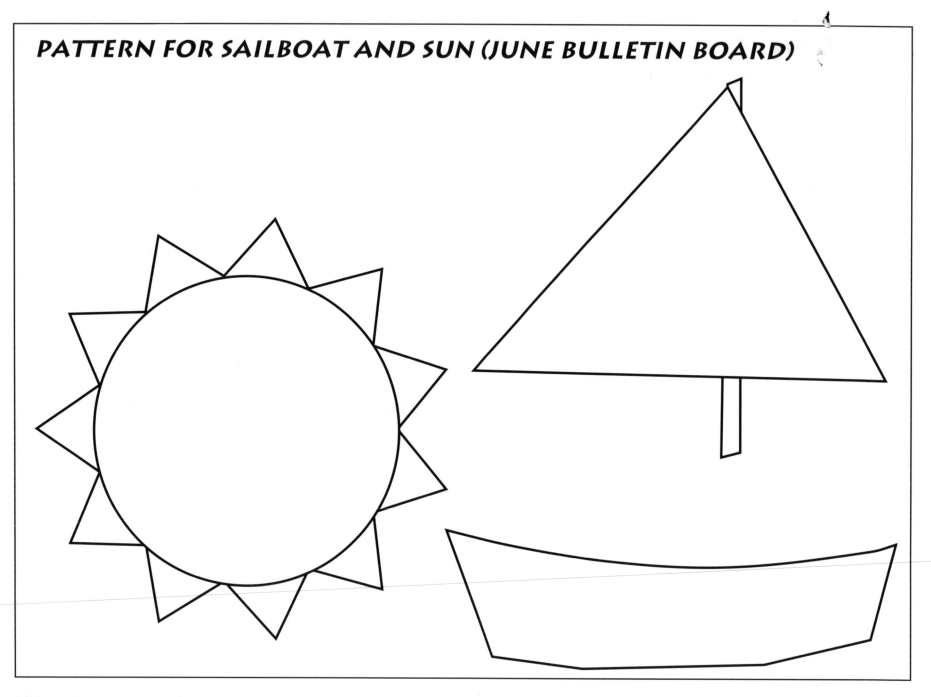

PATTERN FOR ALL-STAR CARDS (USE COVER STOCK PAPER.) (JULY BULLETIN BOARD)

Name_____

Age_____

Height_____ Weight_____ lbs.

Hair_____ Eyes_____

Favorite Food_____

Favorite Color_____

Favorite Bible Story_____

_____

Favorite Bible Character_____

_____

Best Friend_____

Other Important Information_____

_____

Name_____

Age_____

Height_____ Weight_____ lbs.

Hair_____ Eyes_____

Favorite Food_____

Favorite Color_____

Favorite Bible Story_____

_____

Favorite Bible Character_____

_____

Best Friend_____

Other Important Information_____

_____

PATTERN FOR STARS, CIRCLES, AND PRAISE STRIPS (JULY BULLETIN BOARD)

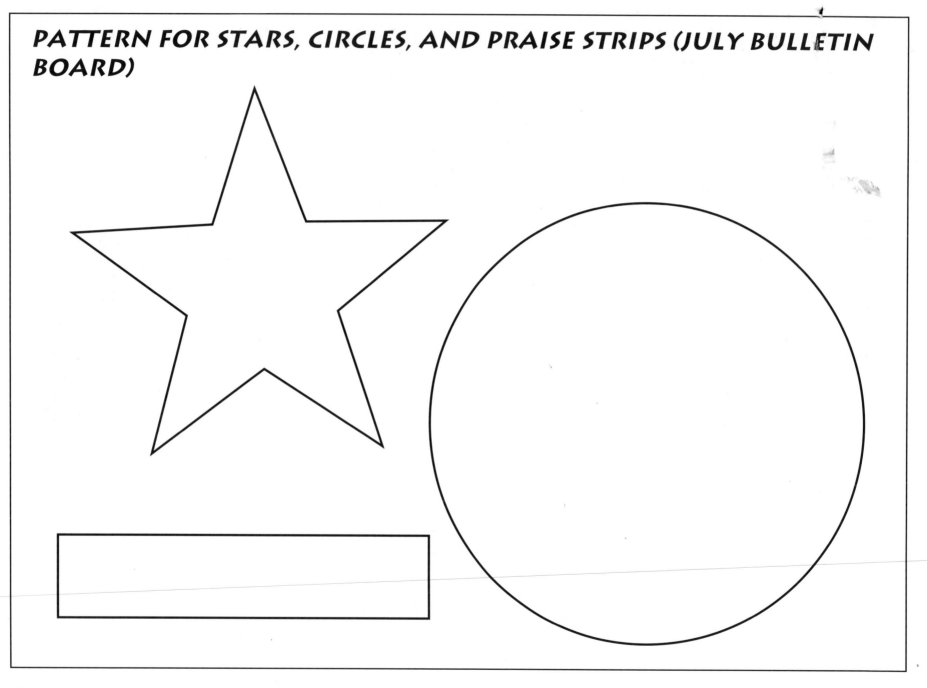

PATTERN FOR BALLOONS (AUGUST BULLETIN BOARD)

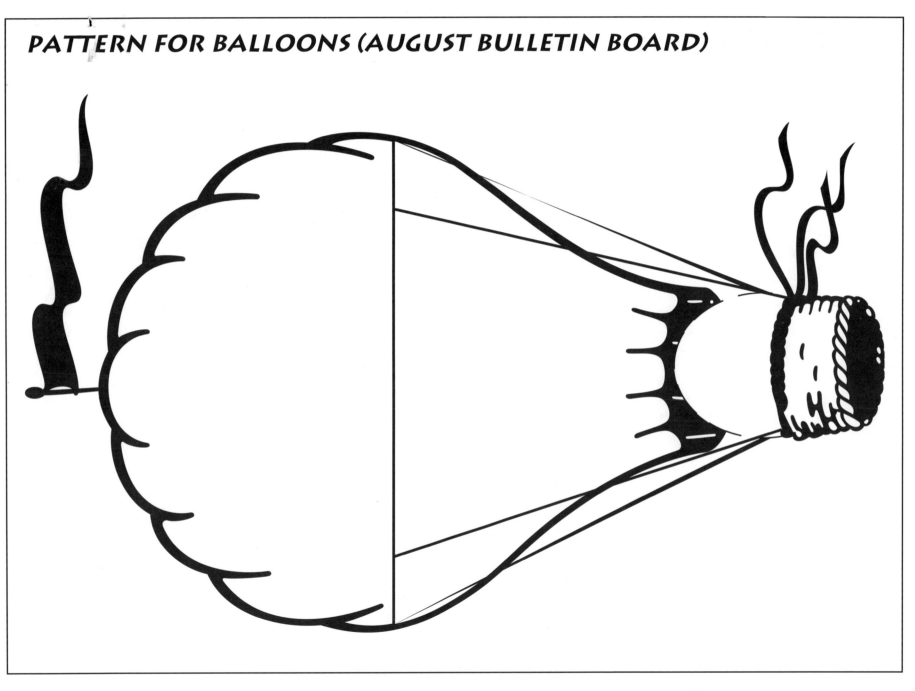

PATTERNS FOR CLOCK (SEPTEMBER BULLETIN BOARD)

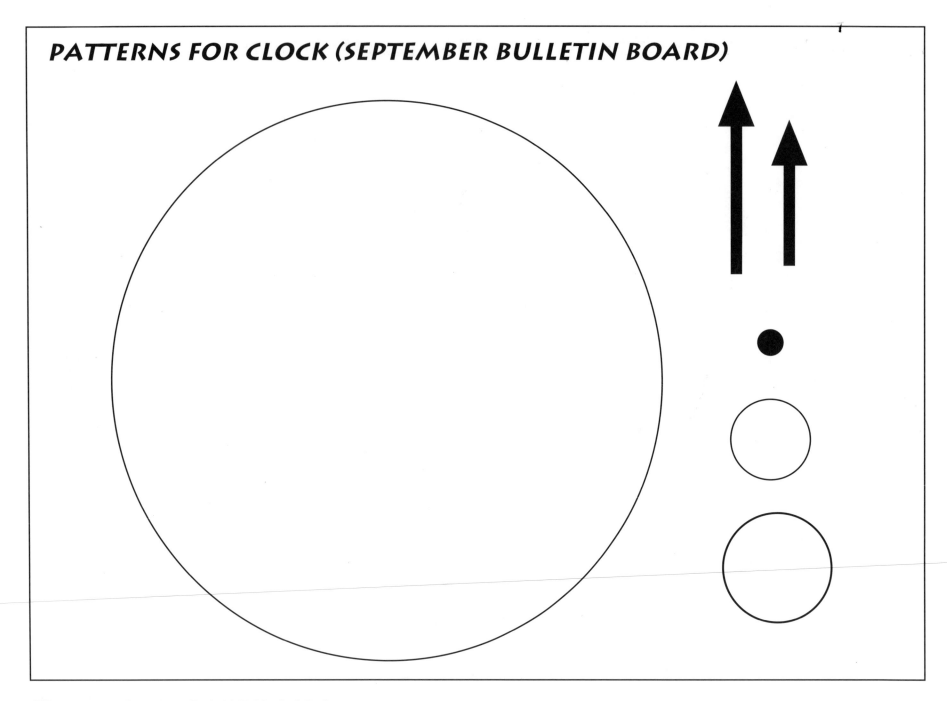

PATTERN FOR SCARECROW (OCTOBER BULLETIN BOARD)

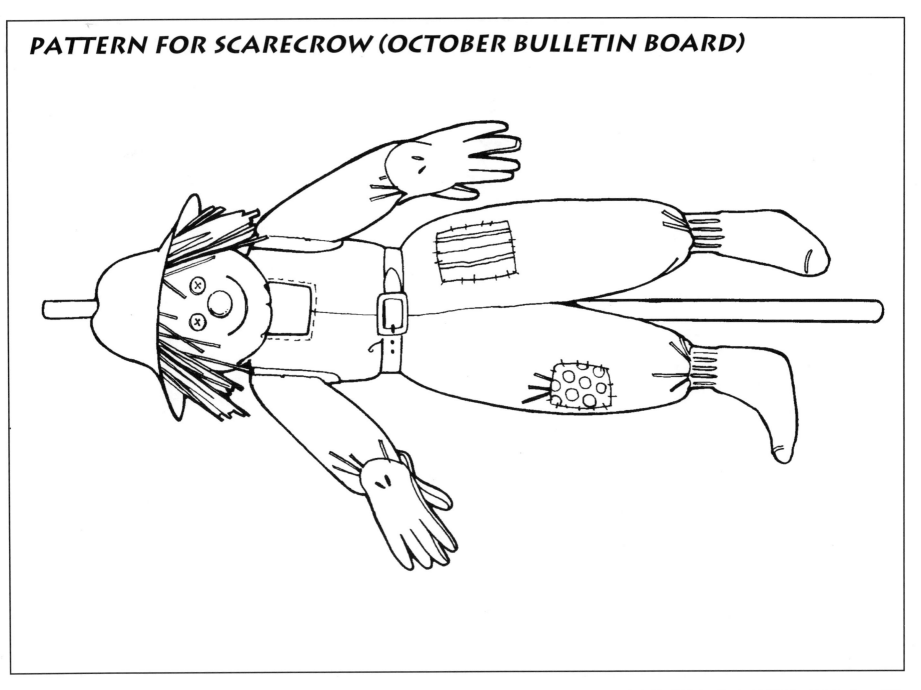

PATTERNS FOR PUMPKINS, LEAVES, BREAD, AND BASKETS (OCTOBER BULLETIN BOARD)

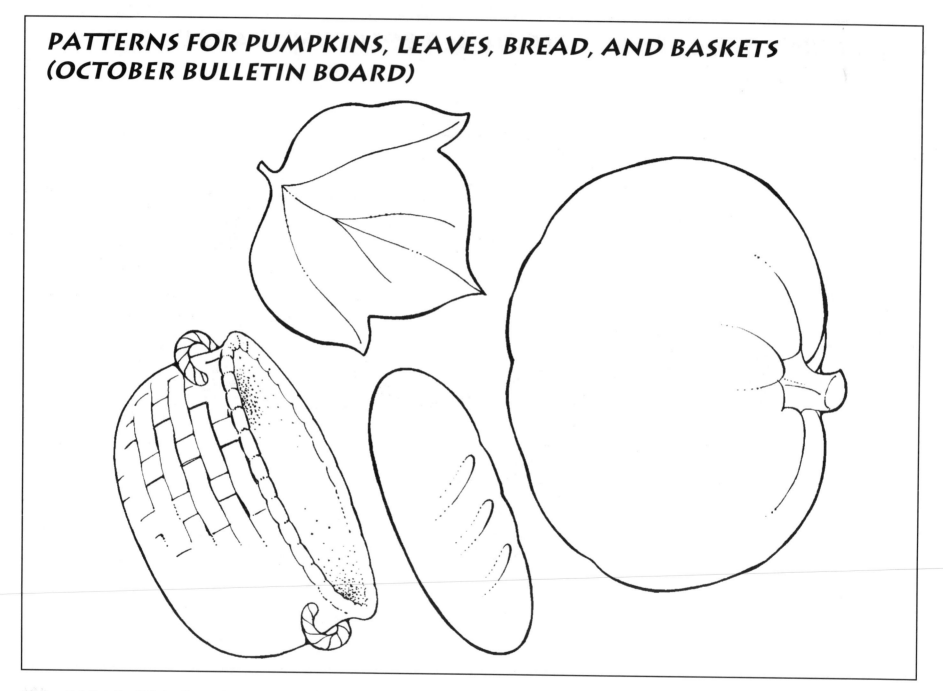

PATTERNS FOR CORNUCOPIA, TURKEY, FEATHERS (NOVEMBER BULLETIN BOARD)

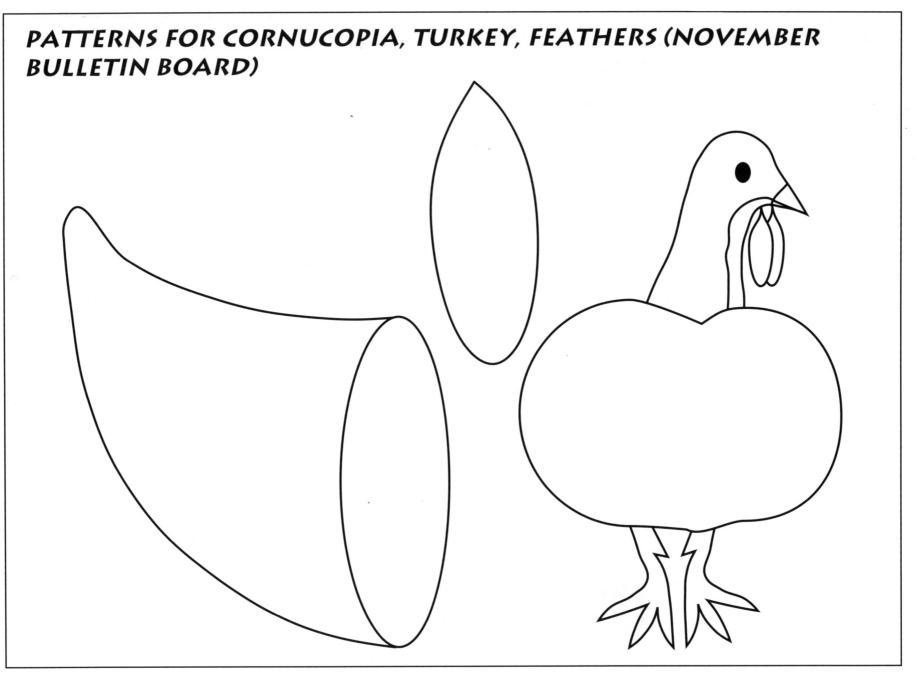

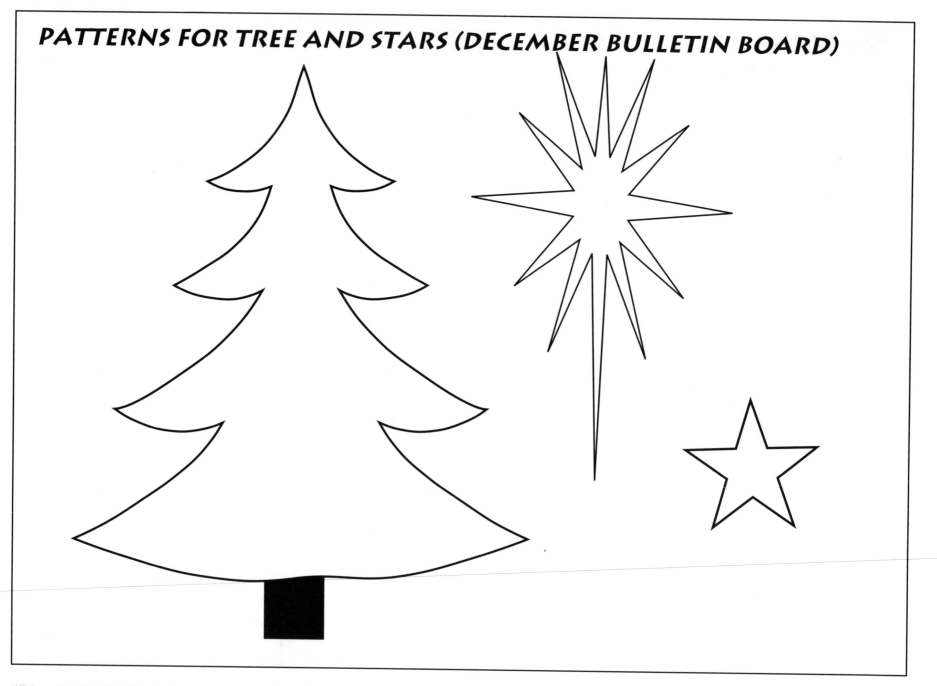

PATTERNS FOR TREE AND STARS (DECEMBER BULLETIN BOARD)

PATTERN FOR CHRISTMAS SYMBOLS

INDEXES

Age Level Index

Topic Index

Scripture Index